AMPLEFORTH COLLEGE

For Rosa and Bill Galliver

AMPLEFORTH COLLEGE

'We Must Look to Ampleforth for the Lead'

The Emergence of Ampleforth College as 'the Catholic Eton'

PETER GALLIVER

GRACEWING

First published in England in 2019
by
Gracewing
2 Southern Avenue
Leominster
Herefordshire HR6 0QF
United Kingdom
www.gracewing.co.uk

The publishers have no responsibility for the
persistence or accuracy of URLs for websites referred
to in this publication, and do not guarantee that any
content on such websites is, or will remain, accurate
or appropriate.

ISBN 978 085244 939 4

Typeset by Word and Page, Chester, UK
Cover design by Bernardita Peña Hurtado

CONTENTS

ACKNOWLEDGEMENTS

I would like to thank my doctoral supervisor at the University of Leeds, Dr Paul Sharp, and Prof. Vincent McClelland of the University of Hull, for their advice on my original research. I am also immensely grateful for the support and assistance given by members of the Ampleforth community, in particular the monastic librarian, Fr Anselm Cramer, and two former headmasters of Ampleforth College, Fr Leo Chamberlain and Fr Wulstan Peterburs. I would also like to thank Jess Farr-Cox for her work in the preparation of my text for publication. The responsibility for all errors is mine.

INTRODUCTION

IN HIS 1944 PUBLICATION on the history of Catholic schools in England, the Cambridge historian H. O. Evennett remarked:

> A detailed critical study of the development of the larger Catholic boarding schools for boys of the upper classes during the past 150 years, placed against the general English social and educational background would constitute a contribution of great value to the history of English Catholicism.[1]

While no such study of all the larger Catholic boarding schools has been undertaken, there has been recent work on The Oratory, Cardinal Newman's attempt to found a school that would provide the Catholic gentry with its own version of Eton.[2] The extent to which the Catholic community required a school comparable to Eton is an important issue in English Catholicism because it says something significant about the integration of English Catholics, or members of its social elite at least, into the British Establishment. Toleration for Catholics in England may have started in the eighteenth century, and Catholic emancipation enacted in 1829, but full engagement of Catholics in the upper reaches of public life had to wait longer.[3] By the last quarter of the nineteenth century, individual Catholics had reached senior positions in the Establishment. For example, Henry Matthews served as Lord Salisbury's Home Secretary and Lord Acton became Regius Professor of History at Cambridge. Facilitating the advance of such Catholics into

---

[1]   H. O. Evennett, *The Catholic Schools of England and Wales* (Cambridge: Cambridge University Press, 1944), p. 64.

[2]   P A Shrimpton, *A Catholic Eton? Newman's Oratory School* (Leominster: Gracewing, 2005).

[3]   The 1778 Relief Act removed some of the restrictions on English Catholics, allowing them greater property rights. The 1791 Toleration Act changed the oath of loyalty to allow Catholics to hold some public offices and legalized schools and chapels. The 1829 Catholic Emancipation Act removed the ban on Catholics in Parliament.

the upper reaches of the professions and state institutions was the quality of their education. Matthews was schooled in Paris, studied at the Sorbonne and completed his degree studies at University College, London.[4] Acton started school in Paris, returned to England to study at Wiseman's Oscott and spent a couple of years in Edinburgh before completing his studies in Munich under one of the leading Catholic theologians, Dollinger.[5] Neither man received the type of public school and university education typical of their peers in political or academic life. By the end of the nineteenth century and into the twentieth, however, wealthy Catholics were educated in schools that were, in effect, English public schools. Catholics advanced into leading positions in professional and public life as integral members of the social class from which the British elite was drawn, rather than as exceptional individuals. This was achieved, not by Catholics sending their sons to the recognized Anglican public schools, but by existing Catholic schools adopting the features that characterized these schools and being accepted as such.

This adaption of Catholic schools via their imitation of the key elements of English institutions helps explain the wider success of the Catholic community in overcoming the legacy of anti-Catholicism stemming from the Reformation era and the isolation of the British Catholic community. This is one of the themes of a recent study by Catherine Pepinster on the relationship between the British and the papacy from the time of John Paul II. The role of education in the integration of Catholics into British society, she notes, worked at every level.

---

[4] Henry Matthews, according to A. Lentin in the *Oxford Dictionary of National Biography*, had a 'varied and cosmopolitan' education. From 1845 he studied at University College, London, graduating in Classics and mathematics in 1847, and in law in 1849. http://www.oxforddnb.com/templates/article.jsp?articleid=34940&back=.

[5] John Dalberg Acton spent 1843 at school in Paris, but from 1843 to 1848 was educated at Oscott under Nicholas Wiseman. He spent two years in Edinburgh under Dr Henry Logan. From 1850 to 1856 he studied in Munich under Prof. Ignaz von Dollinger. Josef L. Altholz, *Oxford Dictionary of National Biography*. http://www.oxforddnb.com/templates/article.jsp?articleid=30329&back.

The elementary schools for the working class (the overwhelming majority of the nineteenth- and early-twentieth-century Catholic community) were under the control of the bishops but followed the model of the state's board schools after 1870, and local authority schools after 1902. The 1944 Education Act saw the Church retain its schools as voluntary aided schools but these, again, followed the model of their state counterparts. Catholic grammar schools became a significant vehicle of social mobility, fuelling a growing Catholic middle class and 'Alongside them, major private schools such as Ampleforth and Stonyhurst became rivals to the Anglican public schools of Eton and Harrow'.[6] In Pepinster's view,

> Catholic schools have made huge achievements and helped create a successful Catholic laity, one that is accepted and even part of the Establishment, and thereby confirmed that the Church to which they belong can be trusted, both in Britain and on the world stage.[7]

It is this Catholic access to the Establishment that is of central importance to this study. A handful of Catholic schools became part of the educational world that played, and continues to play, a fundamental role in the functioning of the British state. The work of Joyce on the social history of the British state has shown how those who ran the British state and its empire were largely formed in the schools developed as public schools in the nineteenth century. These schools were 'miniature universes of the state' in which liberal values were taught alongside lessons in authority, hierarchy and subordination.[8] Public school old boys dominated politics, the armed forces, the civil service and the professions from the second half of the nineteenth century. Their representation in these areas remains disproportionate today. In 2014, the Social Mobility and Child Poverty Commission produced a report showing that seven in ten senior judges, six in ten senior officers in the

---

[6]   C. Pepinster, *The Keys of the Kingdom: The British State and the Papacy from John Paul to Francis* (London: Bloomsbury, 2017), p. 13.
[7]   *Ibid.*, p. 14.
[8]   P. Joyce, *The State of Freedom, A Social History of the British State since 1800* (Cambridge: Cambridge University Press, 2013), p. 265.

armed forces and more than half of the leading figures in the world of the media and the civil service (permanent secretaries and senior diplomats) had been educated in public schools. Sutton Trust figures produced in 2009 showed that 51 per cent of leading medical professionals and 68 per cent of barristers were similarly educated. The same organization found in 2014 that 60 per cent of senior people in financial services came from public schools.[9]

How Catholics fit into this picture, therefore, matters. Given the domination of the English public school world by Eton, it is worth identifying the Catholic equivalent. Whatever the aspirations for the Oratory at its foundation, the school with the best claim to have achieved status amongst Catholic schools as their equivalent of Eton, and to have been accepted in the wider public school world as such, is Ampleforth. This was achieved in the period from the later headmastership of Fr Paul Nevill. Barely a newspaper report or educational publication refers to Ampleforth without making some reference to it and Eton. For example, *The Good Schools Guide* refers to it as 'Eton for Roman Catholics', and a 2003 *Daily Telegraph* article by Graham Turner, while focused on Downside, referred to Ampleforth as 'The Eton of the Catholic world'.[10]

More interesting is what Tim Heald has to say about Ampleforth's place in the public school world from the perspective of supplying members to the networks that dominated British business and public life by the 1980s. He identified the nine leading schools of the 1980s: Ampleforth, Charterhouse, Eton, Harrow, Marlborough, Rugby, Shrewsbury, Westminster and Winchester. For Heald,

> in general network terms—not academic, or social or sporting—it seems to me that these are the only schools

---

[9] See D. Turner, *The Old Boys, The Decline and Rise of the Public School* (Yale: Yale University Press, 2015), pp. 260–1.

[10] A. Atha and S. Drummond, *Good Schools Guide* (London: Lucas Books, 1989), p. 62. G. Turner, 'Faith in the Future', *The Daily Telegraph*, 1 February 2003.

which really count. All others are, like it or not, 'minor' public schools.[11]

A similar perception of Ampleforth's place in the hierarchy of public schools appeared in a *Tablet* article of 1996. Nicholas Pyke wrote:

> There was at one time little doubt that the sons of rich and influential Catholic families went to rich and influential Catholic schools, prominent among them the Jesuit Stonyhurst and, in particular, the Benedictine Ampleforth College. If any school could claim to be a Catholic Eton, Ampleforth in its beautiful isolation amid the North Yorkshire moors, was that school.[12]

The existence of a Catholic college at the pinnacle of the school system favoured by the British establishment was also of importance for the wider Catholic community. It made possible the judgement of Clifford Longley on a key aspect of the significance of Ampleforth's abbot, Fr Basil Hume, a product of Fr Paul Nevill's Ampleforth College, being appointed Archbishop of Westminster in 1976. For Longley,

> The belief that it was possible to be totally English and totally Catholic had been dimmed in what some saw as the 'ghetto years' in the first half of the twentieth century. This was a time when under indifferent leadership (with the possible exception of Cardinal Arthur Hinsley) English and Welsh Catholicism had been allowed to become obsessively inward looking. The remarkable boldness of Pope Paul VI's appointment of the abbot of a Benedictine monastery in North Yorkshire, whose name was associated with one of the best independent boarding-schools in the land, had the power to transform

---

[11] T. Heald, *Networks—Who We Know and How We Use Them* (London. Hodder and Stoughton, 1983), p. 245. Heald's list includes Ampleforth and Marlborough at the expense of Merchant Taylors' and St Paul's from the nine schools considered by the Clarendon Commission as public schools when it began its enquiries in 1861, before reporting in 1864.

[12] See n. 13 below.

both this image and the reality it represented. It revealed
Vatican shrewdness at its best.[13]

Any breaking down of a 'ghetto mentality' in English and
Welsh Catholicism effected by Cardinal Hume, however, did
not work always to his old school's advantage. The context
for Pyke's *Tablet* article was his interest in the extent to which
Catholic families were turning away from Catholic schools and
sending their children to Anglican establishments. His article
was entitled 'Can Eton challenge Ampleforth?'; it pointed out
that, while Lord Longford had been educated at Eton, after his
conversion to Catholicism he had sent his sons to Ampleforth.
The BBC journalist Edward Stourton, from an old Catholic
gentry family and Ampleforth-educated himself, had sent
his sons to Eton, where they could join a Catholic community,
served by Catholic chaplains and worshipping in a Catholic
chapel.[14] This point has also been made by Fr Leo Chamberlain,
a former headmaster of Ampleforth, writing when Master of St
Benet's Hall, Oxford. He argued that Catholic schools had been
successful in enabling Catholics to enter mainstream society
and influence it. As a consequence, a reluctance to welcome
Catholics into the great Anglican schools had faded, to be
replaced by 'an active will to recruit Catholics'.[15]

The extent to which wealthy Catholics have been willing
to respond to the enthusiasm of the great Anglican schools to
recruit their sons is illustrated by the numbers of Catholics
being educated at Winchester and Eton. Winchester appointed
its first Catholic headmaster since the Reformation in 2005
when it recruited Dr Ralph Townsend from Oundle School.
He led Winchester until his retirement in 2016. While Dr
Townsend's son was educated at Ampleforth, the number of
Catholics admitted to Winchester increased under his head-

---

[13]   C. Longley, 'George Haliburton Hume, 1923–1999', *Oxford Dictionary
of National Biography.* http://www.oxforddnb.com/templates/article.
jsp?articleid=72406&back.

[14]   N. Pyke, 'Can Eton Challenge Ampleforth?', *The Tablet*, 18 May 1996.
See also Turner, 'Faith in the Future'.

[15]   Fr Leo Chamberlain, 'Newman the Prophet—Part Two', *Conference
and Common Room*, 44/2 (Summer 2007), p. 12.

mastership. The College currently has between 120 and 130 of its 700 pupils attending Mass on a Sunday morning at one of its two chapels, St Michael's. It has a lay teacher designated as Catholic Chaplain, who leads confirmation classes, and Sunday Mass is said by a priest from Douai Abbey, Woolhampton. In June, the bishop of Portsmouth holds a confirmation service at the school. The school also has the Society of Our Lady of Winton to foster the Catholicism of parents and pupils, present and past.[16]

Eton's Catholic interests are looked after by the St Nicholas at Eton Society. In a school of over 1300, there are in excess of 250 Catholic boys. There has been a resident Catholic chaplain, who is also a priest, since 1985, when Eton had 150 Catholic boys. The first chaplain was Fr Peter Knott SJ and the current incumbent is Fr Nicholas Heap. Mass is said daily in a dedicated Catholic chapel, Lower Chapel. The bishop of Northampton confirms at the school. This is a long way from the state of affairs at the start of the twentieth century. A handful of Catholic gentry families had sent their sons to Eton in the nineteenth century, but the school provided something of a hostile environment to their religion. When Lord Braye purchased land in 1905 to build a chapel for Catholic boys at Eton, the school and the local authority opposed this, and the chapel, Our Lady of Sorrows, was not dedicated until 1915. Eton boys were forbidden by the school from attending Mass there until 1920. The bishop of Northampton had been reluctant to support Braye's plans for a Catholic chapel in Eton, unhappy about Catholic boys being at Eton in the first place.[17]

The 1990s, therefore, represent something of a transition point, when some wealthy Catholics became more willing to send their children to schools to be educated alongside their non-Catholic peers. Catholic boarding schools found it increasing difficult to maintain their numbers faced with this development. There was also the wider issue of parents with

[16] The author teaches at Winchester College. I am grateful to my colleague, the Catholic chaplain, Liam Dunne, for this information.
[17] Taken from the St Nicholas Society website (http://www.stnicholassocietyeton.org).

the resources for private education, whatever their religious affiliation, becoming increasingly reluctant to send their children to boarding schools in the countryside, where term-time visits would be difficult and weekly boarding unviable. This decade saw the closure of the Benedictine schools at Douai and Belmont.[18] Ampleforth's response to a decline in numbers, from around 600 in the 1980s to below 500 by the mid-1990s, saw it follow the example of other boys' schools, such as Marlborough College, and become co-educational. Girls were admitted to the Sixth Form in 2002 and the first 13–18 girls' house, St Margaret's, was opened in 2004.[19] The 1990s also saw a reduction in the monastic community's engagement in the school. The first lay housemaster was appointed to lead one of Ampleforth's ten houses in 1988. By 2014, all housemasters and mistresses were lay and the first lay headmaster had been appointed.[20]

If the willingness of Catholic parents to choose non-Catholic schools and the turn away from rural boarding were not challenge enough, Ampleforth, at the moment, has to confront the consequences of its failings regarding historic child abuse. In 2018, Ampleforth saw its safeguarding procedures deemed inadequate by the Charities Commission and that body imposed its own interim manager to look after safeguarding at the school. The Independent Schools Inspectorate failed the school over its safeguarding practice, and, in consequence, its headmaster was suspended from membership of the Headmasters' and Headmistresses' Conference.[21] As part of its wider

---

[18] Belmont Abbey School closed in 1994. See Dom Simon McGurk and Bishop Mark Jabale, 'The History of Belmont Abbey School', in A. Berry OSB (ed.), *Belmont Abbey, Celebrating 150 Years* (Leominster: Gracewing, 2012), pp. 220–1. Douai closed in 1998. See Abbot Geoffrey Scott, *Centenary History of Douai Abbey* (Woolhampton: Douai Abbey, 2003), p. 35.

[19] Ampleforth College now has three girls' houses: St Margaret's along with two former boys' houses, St Aidan's and St Bede's.

[20] The first lay headmaster was David Lambton. He resigned in 2016 to be replaced by Fr Wulstan Peterburs. The circumstances of his resignation are covered in an article in *The Tablet*, 9 June 2016.

[21] Ampleforth's safeguarding problems and suspension from HMC are covered in an article in *The Tablet*, 24 July 2018.

enquiry into child abuse within the Catholic Church, The Independent Inquiry into Child Sex Abuse, chaired by Prof. Alexis Jay, published on 9 August 2018 a report on Ampleforth and Downside. In some two hundred pages, this detailed instances of abuse and the inadequate response of the authorities within the schools. In Ampleforth's case, the most damning evidence concerned what went on in its preparatory schools, Gilling Castle and Junior House, from the 1960s to the 1980s and the criminal convictions of Fr Gregory Carroll in 2005 and Fr Piers Grant-Ferris in 2006.[22]

In the same month as this report appeared, Pope Francis responded to all such cases of child abuse and cover-ups in the Church by issuing a 'Letter to the People of God'. In this he spoke of 'Crimes that inflict deep wounds of pain and powerlessness, primarily among the victims, but also in their family members and in the larger community of believers and unbelievers alike'. He acknowledged that 'no effort to beg pardon and seek repair will ever be sufficient' but went on to commit the Church to the protection of minors and vulnerable adults. He attacked as 'clericalism' those instances where leaders of religious communities had operated outside legal frameworks to protect abusers and preserve the reputations of their institutions, the sort of practice identified in the Jay Report on the Benedictine schools.[23]

The association of Ampleforth with scandals highlighted by public inquiry, official sanction and Pope Francis's condemnation of clerical abuse led to the *Spectator* carrying the headline 'The End of Ampleforth?' on the front page of its 4 August 2018 edition in reference to an article by Will Heaven.[24] A similar front page appeared on the 18 August edition of *The Tablet* with

---

[22] Independent Inquiry Child Sex Abuse, Ampleforth and Downside (English Benedictine Congregation Case Study) Investigation Report, August 2018. HM Stationery Office, CCS0718147734 08/18

[23] Letter of His Holiness to the People of God, 20 August 2018. http://m. vatican.va/content/francescomobile/en/letters/2018/documents/ papa-francesco_20180820_lettera-popolo-didio.html

[24] Will Heaven, 'A Tale of Two Abbeys', *The Spectator*, 4 August 2018.

an article by Catherine Pepinster under the title 'Ampleforth and Downside: is this the end for Benedictine education?'[25]

In a similar context and vein, Eleanor Doughty in *The Independent* online version, speculated that the abuse scandal might spell the end for 'the so-called Catholic Eton'. In her article, however, she reinforced the perception of Ampleforth as the leading Catholic independent school, observing that 'in the top tier of British boarding schools, some stereotypes remain. The grandest choose Eton, the cleverest Winchester College and the Catholics Ampleforth.'[26]

Ampleforth's response to this most difficult period in its history has been to strengthen the role of lay professionals in the running of the school, while maintaining its commitment to a distinctly Catholic, and Benedictine, education. On 30 August 2018 the Trustees of Ampleforth College announced that Fr Wulstan Peterburs had resigned as headmaster to allow Ms Deidre Rowe, the school's deputy head, to take over as headteacher.[27]

Notwithstanding these difficulties, however, Ampleforth retains support and recognition for the quality of the education it has provided and continues to offer. Sir Julian Brazier, the Conservative Member of Parliament for Canterbury from 1997 to 2017, wrote to the *Sunday Telegraph*, in the wake of the adverse publicity surrounding the school:

> as the parent of boys who attended Ampleforth after the nineties, I am deeply concerned to see the school—and the monks and other staff who played such an important part in the education of my children—being portrayed as they have been. All three of my sons loved their time there. The Benedictine approach involves providing a moral compass, and developing maturity, resilience and care for others.

[25] Catherine Pepinster, 'A Gross Betrayal of Trust', *The Tablet*, 18 August 2018.

[26] Eleanor Doughty, 2018 i article, 'Ampleforth College sexual abuse revelations could spell the the end for the so-called "Catholic Eton"': inews.co.uk/news/education/sexual-abuse-revelations-could-spell-the-end-for-catholic-eton.

[27] *The Tablet*, 8 September 2018.

> From time to time we hear dreadful revelations
> about great national institutions, from Parliament to
> the Church to the NHS. That does not mean we should
> abandon them. Ampleforth is an exceptional school.[28]

This study, however, is concerned not with the present but the past; the period of Ampleforth's emergence as the Catholic equivalent of Eton, at a time when Catholic bishops would not hold confirmation services in Anglican school chapels, and before the crisis precipitated by its failure to deal properly with cases of abuse. This was the period when Catherine Pepinster could write of the Ampleforth monastic community:

> Their school, dubbed the Catholic Eton, educated the
> sons of the poshest and most moneyed Catholic families
> as well as some of the most artistic . . . In the glory days
> of the mid-1970s it was hard to imagine that Ampleforth
> could ever fall from grace.[29]

An exploration of how Ampleforth achieved this position involves a study of the nature of the English public school, the development of Ampleforth as a school within a distinctive Catholic educational tradition in the nineteenth century and its success in becoming the leading Catholic school within the English public school tradition. In the process, this monograph looks at why Catholic schools adopted the characteristics of Anglican public schools and why those Catholics who could afford public schools overwhelmingly patronized these schools rather than Anglican schools, even when the great public schools were willing to accept Catholic pupils. It also considers the tensions that this created within the Ampleforth community by the adoption of the English public school model and why it was Ampleforth rather than any other, in many respects better-placed Catholic schools, that rose to the status of 'the Catholic Eton'.

---

[28] *The Sunday Telegraph,* 19 August 2018.
[29] *The Tablet,* 18 August 2018. The reference to Ampleforth educating some of the more artistic Catholics is explained by former pupils including the sculptor Anthony Gormley, the actor Rupert Everett and writers such as Julian Fellowes and Piers Paul Read.

The English Public School
and English Catholic Education

I F Ampleforth is to be placed within the world of the
English public school, it is important to have some definition of that world. In the literature on the development of
the English public school, however, there is no single agreed
definition of what makes such a school. Each book makes its
own attempt. The most recent, by Turner, starts by quoting the
Master of Wellington College: 'He is a bold man today who
ventures to define what is and what is not a public school',
before venturing a definition of public schools as those free of
state control, drawing their pupils from the elite 10 per cent
of the population able to afford fees and preparing them for
university.[1] Other studies of the development of public schools
have used between six and twelve criteria in their definition
process and membership of the Head Masters' Conference
(HMC) has also been used as a defining characteristic.[2] With-

---

[1]   D. Turner, *The Old Boys, The Decline and Rise of the Public School* (Yale:
    Yale University Press, 2015), pp. xi–xii.
[2]   Notable modern studies of public schools include T. W. Bamford, *The
    Rise of the Public Schools* (London: Nelson, 1967); J. Gathorne Hardy,
    The Public School Phenomenon (London: Penguin, 1977); B. Gardner,
    The Public Schools (London: Hamish Hamilton, 1973); J. R. deS. Honey,
    Tom Brown's Universe (London: Millington, 1977); V. Ogilvie, *The
    English Public School* (London: Batsford, 1957); G. Walford, *Life in
    Public School* (London: Methuen, 1986); and I. Weinberg, *The English
    Public Schools* (New York: Atherton Press, 1967). The study using six
    criteria for the categorizing of public schools was Ogilvie's. He started
    with the Clarendon schools. His approach was adopted by Mangan
    in his study of athleticism in the public schools: see J. A. Mangan,

out becoming embroiled in distinctions between boarding and day schools and attempting to analyse the entire range of schools that might be included in the public school category, the focus in this work is on the elite group within the wider public school world. Simply, this means those schools accepted as major public schools by the Clarendon Commission of 1861 to 1864 and those schools that subsequently achieved something approaching parity of esteem with them. The Clarendon schools, in order of foundation, were Winchester, Eton, Westminster, Rugby, Shrewsbury, Harrow and Charterhouse.[3] Two London schools that were to become predominantly day schools, St Paul's and Merchant Taylors', were also looked at by the Commission, but were not covered by the subsequent Public Schools Act of 1868. Shrewsbury's inclusion was perhaps marginal. An exchange between the cricket captains of Westminster and Shrewsbury in 1866 nicely illustrates this and the extent to which subjective impressions matter in the definition of public schools. The Westminster boy's response to a request for a fixture was that

> Westminster plays no schools except public schools and the general feeling of the school quite coincides with that of the Committee of the Public School Club who issue this list of public schools, Charterhouse, Eton, Harrow, Rugby, Westminster and Winchester.[4]

Notwithstanding this snub, Shrewsbury shared the key feature of the Clarendon schools. They were all ancient foundations and boarding schools patronized by the British elite. Their curriculum was founded on the teaching of Classics and they were organized around the house system. Boys were admitted

---

Athleticism and the Victorian and Edwardian Public School (London: Frank Cass, 1981). Weinberg used twelve criteria. For a discussion of the way in which the literature on public schools handles the issue of definition, see P. W. Galliver, *The Development of Ampleforth College as an English Public School*, unpublished EdD thesis, University of Leeds, 2000, pp.11–18.

[3]   The schools were founded on the following dates: Winchester 1382, Eton 1440, Westminster 1540, Shrewsbury 1552, Rugby 1567, Harrow 1572 and Charterhouse 1611.

[4]   Honey, *Tom Brown's Universe*, p. 240.

to these schools as members of houses. Fifty to seventy boys would live in a house, under a housemaster with the support of a matron (in Eton's case, a dame) and go to the central school buildings for their classes. Schools expanded by the creation of new houses. Crucial to the house system was the standing of senior boys in the Sixth Form and exercise of disciplinary authority by these senior boys over their younger peers. As Honey commented in his discussion of Arnold's development of the Sixth Form and the prefect system at Rugby,

> This helped perpetuate in English schools in the nineteenth century the popular distinction between the terms public and private schools as indicating the difference between schools in which pupils were entrusted to govern themselves through a hierarchy of prefects and fags and schools in which discipline was maintained only by the constant supervision of masters.[5]

This practice of giving boys disciplinary responsibility is a theme of considerable importance in the emergence of schools as public schools. For example, Cotton, when taking over at Marlborough in 1852, informed the governors that he would make the school govern itself by means of prefects or he would resign.[6] The headmaster of Cheltenham, Dobson, said that he did not want his staff supervising boys during their break; constant surveillance

> must have a tendency to destroy or at least weaken the independence and manliness of character, the formation of which is the principal advantage of a large school ... I believe that when boys are trusted much reliance can be placed upon their honour.[7]

Brereton, a founder of public schools for the middle classes, when giving a lecture on the greatness of Arnold of Rugby as an educationalist in 1895, focused on giving responsibility to boys:

[5] *Ibid.*, p. 24.
[6] *Ibid.*, p. 105. The same story is given in R. L. Archer, *Secondary Education in the Nineteenth Century* (London: Frank Cass, 1966), p. 23.
[7] M. C. Morgan, *Cheltenham College, The First One Hundred Years* (London: Sadler, 1961), p. 23. Cited in Honey, *Tom Brown's Universe*, p. 36.

besides the teaching and learning, the daily life of the community is isolated into a boys' world. These evils may be controlled, chastised and to some degree suppressed by constant and effective vigilance of schoolmasters. But they can never be expurgated and replaced by good and healthy life, except by an active spirit of self-government and self-discipline animating the boys' world itself . . . To achieve this was Arnold's great work as headmaster of a great school.[8]

From the second half of the nineteenth century a school could not really claim to be a public school without having the requisite degree of boy authority in its disciplinary structures. A typical example of such a perception in a school's development is provided by A. F. Leach's comment on the history of Warwick School. Attributing to W. Grundy, headmaster 1880–5, 'the re-making of the school along public-school lines', Leach emphasized the establishment of a prefect system.[9]

The final defining characteristic of a public school by the first part of the twentieth century is a commitment to games as an important part of school life. The work of Mangan has shown this development's significance. Those schools that aspired to public school status had to embrace the cult of athleticism. When discussing the development of Lancing, Mangan commented on the extent to which, under Walford as its headmaster, the school shed its emphasis on Anglo-Catholic spirituality to embrace the games ethic. Such an approach made the school a public school and brought an increase in numbers. In Mangan's view, 'Puseyism was forgotten, masculinity emphasized, numbers increased'. He saw this as 'Emulation for acceptance and survival'.[10]

---

[8]   Lecture by J. L. Brereton to Church of England Young Men's Society, King's Lynn, 4 November 1895. Cited in Honey, *Tom Brown's Universe*, p. 61.

[9]   A. F. Leach, *History of Warwick School* (London: Archibald Constable, 1906). Cited in Honey, *Tom Brown's Universe*, p. 32.

[10] J. A. Mangan, *Athleticism*, p. 42. After Newman's conversion to Rome the Oxford Movement broke up. Those Oxford theologians remaining within the Church of England saw themselves as Anglo-Catholics. Pusey was their most prominent figure and Anglo-Catholics were

Ampleforth made its first step across the public school threshold in 1911 when Fr Edmund Matthews was elected to the HMC.[11] The HMC was set up by those schools outside the Clarendon Commission's scope, but these schools had become members within five years and thereafter took a leading role.[12] The matter of Ampleforth gaining acceptance as a leading public school, sitting metaphorically at the top table with the Clarendon schools and the most successful of the new boarding schools, however, cannot be dated so precisely. This had to wait until the headmastership of Fr Paul Nevill. Under his leadership from 1924 to 1954, Ampleforth completed its acquisition of all the accoutrements of an English public school: the house system, prefectorial power, academic success and a commitment to games. Vital to the recognition of Ampleforth as a leading public school, however, was the raising of its social tone by the acquisition of the sons of the Catholic gentry and aristocracy. By the time of Fr Paul Nevill's death in 1954, Ampleforth was counted as a leading public school because of the social composition of its intake and its record in sending its boys on to Oxford, Cambridge and Sandhurst.

sometimes referred to as Puseyites. For Pusey's leading position within the Anglo-Catholic wing of the Church of England, see C. Brad Fraught, *The Oxford Movement* (University Park: University of Pennsylvania Press, 2003), pp. 27–8. Rev Nathaniel Woodard founded, between 1848 and 1869, a network of schools to provide the middles classes with public schools that would promote Anglo-Catholicism. See Honey, *Tom Brown's Universe*, p. 50.

[11] J. McCann, and C. Cary-Elwes, *Ampleforth and its Origins* (London: Burns and Oates, 1952), p. 248.

[12] The first HMC meeting was called by the headmaster of Uppingham, Edward Thring, and held at his school in 1869. The thirteen schools attending were Bromsgrove, Bury St Edmunds, King's Canterbury, Felsted, Lancing, Liverpool College, Norwich, Oakham, Repton, Richmond, Sherborne, Tonbridge and Uppingham. These schools were a mixture of grammar schools whose foundation dated from the Reformation, such as Uppingham, Oakham and Tonbridge, and recently founded schools such as Liverpool College. All wanted to be seen as public schools. J. Lawson and H. Silver, *A Social History of Education in England* (London: Methuen, 1973), p. 303. By 1873, the seven boarding schools of the Clarendon Commission were all involved (Gardner, *Public Schools*, p. 229). The organization became the Headmasters' and Headmistresses' Conference in 2005.

It had, moreover, also made a start in acquiring a reputation as a leading school for rugby football.

The advance made by Ampleforth in the matter of Sandhurst entry is particularly interesting. By the time of Fr Paul's death, the Catholic public schools of Ampleforth and Downside were amongst the leading schools supplying entrants to Sandhurst. The ability of Old Amplefordians and Old Gregorians to mix at Sandhurst with Old Etonians as fellow ex-public schoolboys shows how successful the Catholic schools had been in pushing themselves into the front rank of the English public schools. The following table, taken from Gardner, shows the schools supplying the greatest numbers to Sandhurst in 1891 and 1961.

Schools Supplying Entrants to Sandhurst[13]

	1891		1961
Wellington	37	Wellington	54
Eton	29	Haileybury	21
Clifton	19	Eton	20
Marlborough	16	Ampleforth	17
Harrow	16	Marlborough	16
Haileybury	14	Downside	15

The ability of Ampleforth and Downside to achieve this prominence in Sandhurst entry also says something about the decline of prejudice against Catholics in the twentieth century. The Army, or certain regiments at least, would appear to have provided important opportunities for Catholics to enter the professions acceptable to gentlemen. That Ampleforth would arrive at this position, however, was by no means obvious at the time of its establishment in North Yorkshire.

---

[13]   Gardner, *Public Schools*, p. 182.

2

The Continental Origins
of Ampleforth

HE ORIGINS OF AMPLEFORTH were in the school run by the Benedictine community of St Laurence at Dieulouard in Lorraine. This was one of several foundations established on the continent by English Catholics at the end of the sixteenth and start of the seventeenth centuries, to continue the religious practices outlawed in England, provide the education of the missionary priests necessary for the maintenance of a Catholic community within England during penal times, and to provide a Catholic education for the sons of the Catholic aristocracy and gentry.

At Douai in 1568, Fr William Allen founded an English college that provided for the education of lay boys and the formation of priests for the mission in England. The Jesuits founded a school at St Omers in 1593.[1] The Benedictines established communities in Flanders, St Gregory's, Douai (in 1607), Lorraine, St Laurence's, Dieulouard (in 1608) and Hanover, St Michael's, Lamspringe (in 1643).[2] The Dieulouard community's school was initially a junior seminary for a few boys intended for the priesthood. The Douai and Lamspringe communities opened schools that could accommodate those not intended

---

[1] T. E. Muir, *Stonyhurst College, 1593–1993* (London: Stonyhurst Association, 1993), p. 20.

[2] For Douai and Dieulouard, see C. Almond, *The History of Ampleforth Abbey* (London: R. and T. Washbourne, 1903), p. 48. For Lamspringe, see A. Cramer (ed.), *Lamspringe: An English Monastery in Germany* (St Laurence Papers 7, Ampleforth 2003), p. vi.

for the religious life in 1611.[3] The Dominicans had a school, which, after a troubled beginning in the mid-seventeenth century, operated at Bornhelm in Flanders from 1673.[4]

Of the schools run by orders, the Jesuit school was the largest. Besides educating the boys intended for the Society, the Jesuit school tended to have the largest numbers of sons of Catholic gentlemen who were not intended for the priesthood. Within three years of its opening, the Jesuit school at St Omers had fifty boys. At its peak in 1610, it had 135 pupils. St Omers's numbers fell in the wake of the English Civil War, when the Catholic gentry suffered from its association with the Royalist cause, and the Jesuit school suffered again in the second half of the eighteenth century when the Society of Jesus fell foul of the Church. To continue functioning, the school had to move to Bruges in 1762 and Liege in 1773, before being driven back, as a result of the French Revolution, to a now more tolerant England.[5]

The Benedictine schools were smaller affairs. The numbers at Lamspringe ranged from a low of ten to a high of forty-five; Douai usually had about fifty boys; Dieulouard even fewer.[6] The community at Dieulouard seldom numbered more than sixteen or so. The handful of boys in its school were usually intended for the priesthood. The pattern was for young men to stay at Dieulouard until their ordination and then return to England to work on the missions, mostly in Lancashire. There was a shift in the relationship between St Gregory's and St Laurence's with regard to education in the latter part of the eighteenth century. After a monastic reform of 1761, there was a scheme to have St Gregory's as a common novitiate and house of higher studies. In 1778 it was decided to have the lay school at Dieulouard while taking all novices at St Gregory's. This move appears not to have particularly strengthened

---

[3] Dom Hubert van Zeller, *Downside By and Large* (London: Sheed and Ward, 1954), p. 6.

[4] A. S. Barnes, *The Catholic Schools of England* (London: Williams and Norgate Ltd., 1926), p. 91.

[5] Muir, *Stonyhurst*, p. 20.

[6] For Douai and Dieulouard, see van Zeller, *Downside*, p. 6. For Lamspringe, see Cramer, *Lamspringe*, pp. 105–6.

the school at Dieulouard, while it weakened the school at Douai. Notwithstanding the decision to rationalize educational resources, Dom Jerome Sharrock[7] was loth to see the end of St Gregory's school for lay boys and the school was kept going by the admission of French boys.[8] On the eve of being driven from the continent, therefore, in spite of vicissitudes, the three schools were still functioning.

During their years on the continent, the Jesuit and Benedictine Schools offered a similar sort of education to their pupils. As Fr Cuthbert Almond remarked in his history of Ampleforth, 'The Catholic colleges abroad, before the French Revolution, had so much in common that there is a family likeness in the traditions they brought back to England with them'.[9] All schools kept their boys with them for most of the year. The expense and danger of journeys made frequent visits home imprudent. When at school, the boys were, in effect, members of the religious communities in which they were being educated. Their masters were young men, only just out of the school themselves, completing their final studies before being ordained and sent back to England on the mission. The curriculum and pedagogic methods were different in important respects from those obtaining in the contemporary public schools in Protestant England. The Catholic schools offered a wider educational diet than just the Classics and boys of differing ages and abilities were taught in separate classrooms by their class masters. Catholic schoolboys were regularly tested. There was not the common schoolroom, which was to be found at schools such as Eton, Winchester and Westminster in the seventeenth and eighteenth centuries.

The Jesuit school at St Omers was governed for the majority of the period by the Ratio Studiorum issued for Jesuit schools in 1599.[10] This prescribed in some detail the content of the

---

[7] Jerome (or James) Sharrock was prior of St Gregory's from 1781 until his death in 1808. See Fr Athanasius Allanson OSB, *Biography of the English Benedictines*, ed. Fr Anselm Cramer OSB (Ampleforth: Ampleforth Abbey Trustees, 1999), p. 286.
[8] van Zeller, *Downside*, p. 17.
[9] Almond, *Ampleforth Abbey*, p. 350.
[10] Muir, *Stonyhurst*, p. 24.

curriculum, the structure of the school day and how lessons were to be delivered. Amongst the key elements of the Jesuit prescription for education were that there should be no punishments of boys by boys and that the system should be closely supervised. A 'prefect of discipline' would be responsible for order in the school. Boys were to be supervised at all times. Academic work would come under the supervision of a 'prefect of studies'. The various classes were to be regularly examined by the Prefect of Studies to monitor their progress. Pastorally at St Omers, the boys were grouped according to age in Playrooms. Besides this grouping, boys were also organized into prayer groups known as sodalities. The first sodality was established in 1609.[11]

Things were similar in the Benedictine schools. Educational life was not governed by the Ratio Studiorum, but there were prefects of studies and discipline appointed from members of the monastic communities to run the schools; there were separate masters and classrooms; and there was regular testing of pupil progress. An example of the approach of the Benedictines to their schools in this period is provided by the notes on education written by Dom George Augustine Walker, President of the English Benedictines from 1777 to 1790. In these, there is a consideration of both the content and methods of a good education. Walker saw a place for physical education and, in the teaching of religion, history was to play a role; not just sacred history, but also 'that of a child's own country should be read'.[12] There is an indication that at St Gregory's, Douai, the curriculum may have been overly focussed on the Classics in relation to other Catholic schools. In 1736, the Grand Prior of Arras, following a visitation, instructed the monks of St Gregory's to include modern languages and mathematics in their curriculum.[13] There is at least one indication, however, that St Gregory's offered a good standard of schooling. Gilbert Langley had spent time at Charterhouse and was also

---

[11] *Ibid.*, p. 31.
[12] Walker's views on education are discussed in Cramer, *Lamspringe*, pp.110–12.
[13] van Zeller, *Downside*, p. 16.

educated at Douai from 1721 to 1726.[14] His recollection was that the standard of teaching at Douai, where 'the scholars are divided according to their different abilities and capacities into several classes and over each class presides a proper master', was higher than that obtaining in the English school.[15]

The Catholic schools developed their own games. St Omers had its own version of cricket. The students from Douai brought with them to Ushaw a bat and ball game called cat.[16] The Benedictine schools played horniholes, or own-y-holes, a game that, from a copy of the rules transcribed at Ampleforth in 1912, appears to have been something of a cross between cricket and rounders.[17] All of the schools had ball walls for playing a game similar to racquetball. In the near two hundred years spent on the continent, therefore, the Catholic schools developed distinctive educational traditions that they were to bring with them on their return to England.

14   *Ibid.*, p. 13.
15   J. Gathorne Hardy, *The Public School Phenomenon* (London: Penguin, 1977), p. 34.
16   Barnes, *Catholic Schools*, p. 139.
17   Ampleforth Abbey Archives, BX51–1, p. xi.

3

Ampleforth and the Catholic Colleges

The Return to England
and the Early Nineteenth Century

T HE REMNANTS OF THE CATHOLIC COMMUNITIES fleeing the French Revolution did not return to an England in which there was no provision for the education of Catholics. The establishment of Catholic schools and functioning of Catholic schoolmasters was forbidden by law, but Catholic schools had existed in penal times. Discreetly run Catholic schools could be accorded tacit toleration in the eighteenth century. These were small establishments often dependent upon an individual teacher. In the first half of the eighteenth century, for example, there was a Catholic school at Twyford.[1] In the 1740s, there was a school at Rowney Wood in Worcestershire run by Fr Palin[2] and a school at Edgbaston, Warwickshire, run by Franciscans.[3] In Lancashire, there was a

---

[1] Barnes, *Catholic Schools*, p. 97. Barnes mentions that Twyford's principal claim to fame was having Alexander Pope amongst its pupils. Barnes also writes that in 1726 the school was run by Mr Fleetwood, a secular priest, and had over a hundred boarders. There is no Fr Fleetwood in either A. Bellenger, *English and Welsh Priests 1558–1800* (Downside: Downside Abbey Books, 1984), or C. Fitzgerald-Lombard, *English and Welsh Priests 1801–1914* (Downside: Downside Abbey Books, 1993), who matches Barnes's description.

[2] Rowney Wood is mentioned in F. C. Husenbeth, *The History of Sedgley Park School* (London: Richardson and Son, 1856), p. 5. A Fr Richard Palin, 1670–85, is recorded in Bellenger, *English and Welsh Priests*, p. 93.

[3] Barnes, *Catholic Schools*, p. 108.

school at Fernyhalgh, near Preston, chiefly for the sons of the nobility and gentry, known as 'Dame Alice's' after its founder Alice Harrison, or 'Ladywell'.[4]

Towards the end of the eighteenth century, Bishop Challoner was influential in the establishment of schools that were to prove long lasting. In 1763, a school was established in the midlands at Sedgley Park and in 1769 a school was founded at Old Hall Green in Hertfordshire. Both were modelled on the English College at Douai. By 1764, the school at Sedgley Park had 51 entrants and by the end of the eighteenth century the overall numbers in the school were between 90 and 100.[5] When founded, these schools were still technically outside the law, but they were able to exist in an atmosphere of tacit, limited toleration. The first Catholic Relief Act was not passed until 1778, and even the more wide-ranging Second Relief Act of 1791, which removed sanctions against Catholic schoolmasters, was still ambiguous with regard to the establishment of Catholic schools. Notwithstanding this, by the time of the French Revolution, the way was open for the return of Catholic schools and colleges from the continent and the expansion of Catholic education in England.[6]

Members of the English College at Douai returned to stimulate the development of an existing Catholic establishment, and to found a new one. In February 1894, twenty-one exiles from Douai settled at Old Hall in Hertfordshire. Overcrowding at Old Hall, which in 1795 became St Edmund's College, led to members of the Douai community looking for a new foundation in the Northern District. After brief spells at Tudhoe and Crook Hall, a permanent site for the college was found at Ushaw. Building started in 1804 and completed in 1809, when the College (under Fr Thomas Eyre) had eighty students. By

---

4   *Ibid.*, p. 108. The headmaster at 'Dame Alice's' from 1744 to 1754 was Dr George Kendal, brother of Fr Richard Peter Kendal OSB, who was the prior who arranged for the transfer of the community of St Gregory, and its school, to Downside. *Ibid.*, p. 192.

5   Husenbeth, *Sedgely Park*, p. 20.

6   For a discussion of the development of the law relating to Catholic schools, see D. A. Milburn, *History of Ushaw College* (Durham: Ushaw Bookshop, 1964), p. 27.

1811, the College had 130 students and, as at Douai, educated both clerical and lay students.[7]

Of the returning schools run by religious orders, it was the Jesuit foundation at Stonyhurst that was the first to become firmly established. The Jesuits returned to England in 1794 and were able to settle in a country house at Stonyhurst provided by Sir Thomas Weld. It operated on a larger scale than the Benedictine schools, educating a higher proportion of boys not intended for religious life and extending the range of its studies into higher education with its Philosophers. The least successful of the returning schools was that of the Dominicans. The Dominicans had set up a school at Carshalton in Surrey in 1793 and it was to there that the remnants of the Bornhelm school went. By 1811, however, the Carshalton school, despite having around fifty pupils, was in severe financial trouble and was closed.[8] Following the closure of Carshalton, the Dominicans ran what Barnes called 'a struggling little school'[9] at Hinckley until it too closed in the mid-century. The Dominicans did not run a successful school until the opening of a new school at Hinckley in 1884, subsequently transferred to Hawkesyard, then Laxley Hall.[10]

The Jesuit school at Stonyhurst was run on much the same lines as the St Omers school. An indication of how important continuity with the continental school was to the Jesuits was the building of a handball wall for the boys as early as 1796.[11] As at St Omers, the boys remained organized in playrooms and taught in separate classrooms. Discipline remained strict. Boys were under constant supervision and rules fiercely enforced. In 1847, the *Preston Guardian* ran a report on the severity of the floggings administered at Stonyhurst.[12] Like many schools in this period, the numbers at Stonyhurst could fluctuate quite wildly.[13] Initially the school did well and, after the worldwide

---

[7]   *Ibid.*, pp. 107–11.
[8]   Barnes, *Catholic Schools*, pp. 94–5.
[9]   *Ibid.*, p. 95.
[10] *Ibid.*
[11] Muir, *Stonyhurst*, p. 76.
[12] *Ibid.*, p. 91.
[13] See Honey, *Tom Brown's Universe*, pp. 144–5, for examples of the fluctuating fortunes of schools in the first half of the nineteenth century.

restoration of the Jesuits by Pius VII in 1814, attracted over a hundred pupils. There was a setback, however, in the early 1820s. After 1818, the Jesuits were preoccupied with a dispute over their right to present candidates for ordination to a bishop other than the local bishop. According to Muir, the most recent historian of Stonyhurst College, this period saw a perceived deterioration in discipline and academic standards that saw numbers fall.[14] By 1824, however, there had been a recovery. According to an advertisement in the *Blackburn Mail*, the Stonyhurst of that year had three playrooms, six schoolrooms and a study place for 220 scholars.[15] The capacity of the schoolroom was not realized, but by 1843 the school had 183 pupils.[16]

While Stonyhurst was establishing itself, the schools of the Benedictines operated on a smaller scale. Handfuls of monks from both communities escaped from France during the Revolution. Both communities had trouble finding permanent residences on their return. The Dieulouard community found temporary homes in Lancashire, its historic source of recruitment and the principal region of its missionary work. For a time, in 1795, the communities of St Gregory from Douai and St Laurence's, Dieulouard, shared accommodation at the house of Sir Edward Smythe at Acton Burnell. The communities, however, were determined to maintain their separate identities and the co-residential experience did not prove a success. Sir Edward Smythe had been educated at St Gregory's and it was the St Laurence monks who moved out of Acton Burnell. After short stays in several Lancashire locations, the community of St Laurence in 1802 took up permanent residence in Ampleforth Lodge, Yorkshire, the retirement house provided by Lady Anne Fairfax for her chaplain, Fr Anselm Bolton, a monk of Dieulouard.[17]

The community of St Gregory was not able to stay at Acton Burnell. On Sir Edward Smythe's death in 1811, the monks

[14] *Ibid.*, p. 85.
[15] *Ibid.*, p. 75.
[16] *Ibid.*, p. 86.
[17] For details of attempts by the St Laurence community to find a permanent home, see McCann and Cary-Elwes, *Ampleforth and its Origins*, pp. 205–9.

were displaced. A permanent settlement, however, was found at Downside in Somerset. Invited to settle in the Western Province by Bishop Peter Bernardine Collingridge, the community of St Gregory found the £7338 required to purchase Downside House in 1814.[18]

At both Ampleforth and Downside, schools were established shortly after the monastic communities became settled. Both schools were small-scale affairs and predominantly concerned with the education of boys intending to join the community. The school at Downside in 1814 had twelve boys, eight of whom were to become monks. By 1818, the number at Downside had risen to 24. From 1830 to 1845, the numbers were steady at 36, with sixty being reached in 1854 when a new school block was opened.[19]

Ampleforth was not originally intended to educate boys other than those expecting to ender the religious life. The plan of the President of the Congregation, Fr Bede Brewer, was that Ampleforth should be an exclusively monastic community, while Catholic lay boys were to be educated in Lancashire at the Benedictine school established earlier at Parbold. The Parbold school was derived from a small school for the sons of the gentry founded in 1789 by Fr Gregory Cowley[20] at Vernon Hall. The last prior of Dieulouard, Fr Richard Marsh,[21] had taken control of this school in 1797 and then moved it, and the Community of St Laurence, to Parbold in 1802.[22] When plans to move the community of St Laurence to Yorkshire were being made, Fr Bede Brewer had written:

---

[18] van Zeller, *Downside*, p. 26.

[19] *Ibid.*, p. 40.

[20] Fr Gregory Cowley had been professed at St Laurence's some time before 1749. He was elected prior of St Laurence's in 1765. He was elected President of the English Benedictines in 1794 and in that year took over the management of the school at Vernon Hall near Liverpool. See Allanson, *English Benedictines*, pp. 251–2.

[21] Fr Richard Marsh was professed at St Laurence's in 1783. He was elected prior in 1789 and brought the community to England in 1793. *Ibid.*, pp. 363–5.

[22] *Ibid.*, p. 367.

I wish the school in Lancashire to continue as it is established though on a different plan. I would not admit to Ampleforth any boys other than such as the parents are willing, if they have a vocation, to take the Church.[23]

The beginnings of Ampleforth as a school for boys intended for the religious life can be seen in a letter of 1803 from Fr Brewer to Mrs Metcalf regarding the education of her sons, John and Edward, both of whom did join the community.[24] The letter details the financial provisions for the arrangement. In total, £450 was to be paid,

But in case the said sons or either of them should not choose or not be judged by the Master of Ampleforth Lodge School proper and fit to enter on any ecclesiastical state of life, or if the school should be discontinued or could not maintain itself at the present state of its pensions . . . this will be deducted at the rate of £25 per annum from the time entered into the school.[25]

The plan to keep Ampleforth free from lay boys, however, was abandoned in 1805 when the school at Parbold was broken up and its parents offered a transfer of their sons to Ampleforth.[26] This gave the nascent school at Ampleforth the boost of a

---

[23] Cited in McCann and Cary-Elwes, *Ampleforth and its Origins*, p. 213.
[24] Edward Metcalfe, born in Yorkshire in 1792, was professed as Br Placid in 1811. As Fr Placid, he was sub-prior in 1818 and cellarer in 1822. He left Ampleforth in 1830 to participate in Bishop Baines's plan for Prior Park. He fell out with Baines and unsuccessfully applied to return to Ampleforth. He spent the rest of his life on mission work, dying in Leeds during a typhus outbreak in 1843. See Allanson, *English Benedictines*, pp. 388–9.
[25] Ampleforth Abbey Archives, A267 7G Letter 1, Letter from Fr Bede Brewer to Mrs Metcalf. Fr Bede Brewer was a monk of Dieulouard and EBC President from 1799 to 1822. An account of his life is given in A. Cramer, *Ampleforth, The Story of St Laurence's Abbey and College* (Ampleforth: St Laurence Papers V, Ampleforth Abbey, 2001), pp. 54–7. He also appears in Allanson, *English Benedictines*, pp. 300–8.
[26] Almond, *History of Ampleforth Abbey*, p. 281. Parents of boys at Parbold were given notice of the intention to close the school and offered Ampleforth as an alternative at Christmas 1803. See Allanson, *English Benedictines*, p. 368.

connection with the gentry families who had patronized the Parbold school.

The background to this, and fundamental to the transformation and success of its early school, was the accession to the Ampleforth community of the remnants of the suppressed English Benedictine community of Lamspringe in Hanover.[27] When the monastery at Lamspringe was suppressed by the Prussian government in 1803, President Brewer, notwithstanding his earlier views about the character of the school to be created at Ampleforth, arranged for the remnants of the German school to be settled in Yorkshire. Ampleforth's Prior Appleton[28] met the Lamspringe party at Hull and invited them to join his new house. Leading the party of exiles was Clement Rishton, who had already completed his novitiate. He was now professed for St Laurence's. Twelve boys, aged between twelve and nineteen, accompanied Rishton. Of this group, Peter Baines, Henry Brewer, Edward Glover, Vincent Glover, William Malone, John Molyneux and Thomas Rooker became monks at Ampleforth. John Burchall, John Glover, Robert Latham, Robert Smith and Charles Woods remained in the laity.[29] The Lamspringe school also provided Ampleforth

---

[27]   V. A. McClelland, 'School and Studies in Lamspringe', in Cramer, *Lamspringe*, pp. 103–21.

[28]   Thomas Appleton, Fr Anselm Appleton, had been professed at Dieulouard in in 1788. He escaped just before the seizure of the monastery by the French authorities in 1793. After working in missionary parishes in England, he was elected prior of St Laurence's, Ampleforth, in 1802. According to Allanson, he was 'a strict religious man but his rough ways, combined with a sour temper, were not suited to give satisfaction to others and his community gladly embraced the opportunity of superseding him at the next chapter of 1806'. He spent the next thirty years on the mission at Hindley. He died in 1842. See Allanson, *English Benedictines*, p. 363.

[29]   The list of the Lamspringe boys is recorded in the diary of a Lamspringe monk, Fr Augustine Birdsall. See Cramer, *Ampleforth*, p. 38. The diary itself is kept at Downside Abbey, Downside MS 250. Baines's career at Ampleforth and elsewhere is dealt with in this chapter. The most recent biography is P. J. Gilbert, *This Restless Prelate: Bishop Peter Baines, 1786–1843* (Leominster: Gracewing, 2006). Of the other members of the party, John Molyneux became Fr Alban in 1808 and was sent on the mission to Knaresborough. He was

with its first teaching resources. In 1803, a consignment of 181 Latin and 41 Greek texts, a variety of devotional books and a number of English and Latin grammars, was dispatched from the dissolved house.

Notwithstanding the educational value of the books sent from Hanover to Yorkshire, it was a member of the party of boys who landed at Hull, Peter Baines, who was to have the greatest impact on the early years of the school at Ampleforth. He was professed as a member of the St Laurence community, taking Augustine as his monastic name. At Ampleforth, he became prefect of the school,[30] doing much to shape its character. When he left Ampleforth to assist in the Western Province he continued to promote the school. As a result of his influence, Ampleforth College courted the Catholic gentry with some success. By 1830, although a small school, Ampleforth was, from the perspective of its curriculum, teaching methods, educational attainments and relationships between staff and pupils, an exceptionally good school by the standards of its day, arguably by any standards.

At the heart of Baines' plans for Ampleforth was the adoption of the teaching methods advocated by Prof Gregor von

President of the EBC from 1850 to 1854. See Cramer, *Ampleforth*, p. 74. Of the three Glover brothers, Edward and Vincent became monks. Edward became Br Benet in 1804 and was ordained in1808. He died in 1834. See Allanson, *English Benedictines*, pp. 332–4. Vincent was professed as a monk in 1807 as Br Joseph and was ordained in 1807. Like his brother, he worked on the mission at Knaresborough, dying at Brownedge in 1840. *Ibid.*, pp. 361–2. Thomas Rooker became Fr Cuthbert. He followed Baines to Prior Park, eventually becoming a parish priest at Clifton until his death n 1857. He has an obituary in *The Tablet*, 30 May 1857. Henry Brewer, nephew of President Brewer, became Fr Anselm. He was responsible for the building of a new church at Brownedge and the foundation of a new parish in Liverpool, St Anne's. *Ibid.*, pp. 392–424. William Malone became Fr Boniface. He renounced his vows in 1810 and later married. *Ibid.*, p. 444.

[30] Catholic schools operated by the religious orders on the continent and on their return to England did not have headmasters. There was a prefect of studies, in overall charge of the school, and a prefect of discipline. Both came under the authority of the head of the community.

Feinaigle. Feinaigle was a one-time German monk. He had been professed for the Cistercian monastery of Salem in 1780 but had reverted to the life of a layman in 1804 when the monastery was dissolved. He published his first paper on how the memory might be trained in 1804 and in 1807 he acquired some fame in France through a series of public lectures and demonstrations. When challenged as to the efficacy of his teaching methods Feinaigle had twelve of his pupils offer a demonstration before an audience of two thousand.[31] Feinaigle's method, based on mnemonics, was derived from memory training exercises developed by Cicero and Quintilian. In essence, the system worked through the training of the memory by association. Students had to envisage a town with districts and houses. Districts would be associated with broad topics, while individual facts would be associated with locations within houses. In every district there would be ten houses and within every house a hundred memory places. The date 1436 would be remembered by recalling the 36th quadrate of the fourth room of the first house of the historic district.[32] Using this technique Feinaigle claimed to be able to produce from previously uneducated children prodigious feats of memory. Feinaigle went on to argue that the ease with which his students could memorize information would make possible a far wider range of studies than envisaged by his contemporary educationists. He was also opposed to underpinning the teaching of children with the sanction of force, preferring to encourage his pupils by a system of rewards.

Feinaigle visited England in 1811, speaking in London (where his venues included the Royal Institution and the Surrey Institution), Edinburgh, Glasgow and Liverpool. Feinaigle's visit to England saw his lectures attended by members of fashionable society. In London, one of his hosts had been

---

[31] There is a manuscript account of Feinaigle's life by Thompson Cooper in the Ampleforth Abbey Archives, DX31 7G14, Item 8.

[32] Feinaigle's system is described in some detail in M. Quane, 'The Feinaiglian Institution, Dublin', *Dublin Historical Record*, 19/2 (March 1964), pp. 30–44. The 1436 example is given on p. 31.

Lord Spencer and Lady Derby was in the audience.[33] There is some evidence that his ideas influenced Faraday[34] and there was a degree of interest expressed by Samuel Butler, the head-master of Shrewsbury.[35] Byron, whose personal physician was the Ampleforth-educated John Polidori, made a mocking reference to Feinaigle in Don Juan.[36] The greatest practical impact of Feinaigle's talks, however, was on the English Benedictine Congregation. Fr Bede Brewer was persuaded by Feinaigle and Fr Augustine Baines was encouraged to implement the mnemonic system at Ampleforth. Feinaigle spent time at Ampleforth in 1811 before eventually moving on to Ireland and setting up his own school in Dublin.

The enthusiasm with which Feinaigle's methods were embraced by Fr Augustine Baines can be seen in a letter sent to Feinaigle in Ireland in 1813: 'Your system is completely established in the college . . . our expectations are not disappointed, on the contrary, in most instances they have been exceeded'.[37] As Laver, a modern analyst of Feinaigle's educational method, has commented,

> It flourished as the key to the teaching method [at Ampleforth] for twenty years and was in partial use for fifteen more, probably giving way to traditional methods of instruction because teachers who did not truly comprehend Feinaigle's master plan gradually modified it . . . Certainly the chronologies, classificatory systems and rote learning that were so characteristic of

33 Ampleforth Abbey Archives, Q5–11, Account of Feinaigle's talk. I am indebted to Fr Terence Richardson for this reference. Fr Terence is responsible for a collection of material relating to Feinaigle kept in the Ampleforth Abbey Archives, Q5–11.
34 For the influence on Faraday see E. Hare, 'Michael Faraday's Loss of Memory', *Proceedings of the Royal Institution*, 49 (1976), pp. 33–52.
35 Butler wrote to his connection in Liverpool, William Roscoe, on 28 October 1811 for his views on Feinaigle. Liverpool Local History Library, Roscoe Collection, 604, 605. Copy kept in Ampleforth Abbey Archives, Q05–11.
36 Lord George Gordon Byron, *Don Juan* (London: John Murray, 1818), Canto 1: 11(5).
37 Ampleforth Abbey Archives, Q05–11, Baines Letter to Feinaigle, 23 February 1813.

early nineteenth century education in England must
have seemed less tedious and foreboding at Ampleforth
than elsewhere.[38]

Feinaigle's ideas reinforced the existing disposition of the
school at Ampleforth, modelled on the practices of the Benedictine schools in continental exile, towards broadly based
studies. Ampleforth students in the 1810s, therefore, learnt
Hebrew, Greek, Latin, French, history, geography, natural history, arithmetic and geometry. These subjects were delivered
according to what the Ampleforth examination programme of
1817 called 'the system of Universal Grammar', which 'enables
the student to discover of himself what is irregular or peculiar in each individual language'.[39] This Ampleforth education, which habituated 'the youthful mind to close attention,
cool abstraction and accurate reasoning',[40] was energetically
promoted by Fr Baines. In *The Laity's Directory* of 1815, the
school at Ampleforth was advertised by its curriculum being
published in detail. It was claimed that

> it will not be difficult to appreciate the merits of a
> system which, while it renders the classical part of
> education more extensive, combines at the same time
> every principal branch of useful education, and enables a
> young man, on quitting the college, to appear in society
> with the solid learning of a scholar as well as the elegant
> accoutrements of a gentleman.[41]

Baines reinforced this advertising with his own efforts to
persuade influential Catholic families to send their boys to
Ampleforth. From 1817, he was based in Bath as the incumbent of the Benedictine Mission there. He acquired a reputation as a preacher of some distinction. In 1823 he was
consecrated Coadjutor Bishop to the Vicar Apostolic of the

---

[38] B. Laver, 'Gregor Feinaigle, Mnemonist and Educator', *Journal of the
History of Behavioural Sciences*, 15/1 (January 1979), p. 23.

[39] Ampleforth Abbey Archives, EX01–5.

[40] *Ibid.*

[41] Ampleforth Abbey Archives, EX01–2. Also cited in Almond,
Ampleforth, pp. 290–1.

Western District, the Vicariate, to which he succeeded in 1829.[42] In Bath, Baines had access to gentry families and he can be seen using this on Ampleforth's behalf. Baines had been to Bath even before his appointment to lead the mission. From there, in 1816 he wrote to Prior Rishton at Ampleforth of the success he had found in recruiting boys for the school and exhorting the prior to keep faith with the Feinaigle method if Ampleforth were to eclipse Stonyhurst as the leading Catholic school. In January 1816, the prior was informed that a Mrs Aranzer had taken her son from Downside and would send him to Ampleforth. A Mr Knapp would also send his sons. Fr Baines went on to say:

> When in Lancashire last I had a long dispute amongst a large number of opponents in favour of our system in which Mr. Brindle joined me ... I hope that this information will give you pleasure and convince you ... that if you can continue to make the studies successful you will never want students of the first respectability ... But take care not to quit your ground or lower your pretensions—your forces must consist of deserters from the camp of the Jesuits of which there will always be a great number so long as you go upon different and better principles—but Ampleforth will have no attraction if once it place itself on the same footing as other places of more note.[43]

In 1820 Baines was able to report more success and at the expense of Stonyhurst. Ampleforth had recruited Henry and Edward Clifford from the Jesuit school. These were the younger brothers of Lord Arundell of Wardour, and Henry his potential heir. The acquisition of the Clifford brothers gave Baines an opportunity to voice his opinion of a Stonyhurst education when he wrote that 'As has happened to many others at that establishment he has contrived to acquire little more than a disgust from some branches of his studies, yet not

---

[42] McCann and Cary-Elwes, *Ampleforth*, p. 219.
[43] Ampleforth Abbey Archives, A267 7G39, Letter 2, Baines to Rishton, 13 January 1816.

nearly in so great a degree as Edward Clifford'.[44] For Baines
the recruitment of gentry and aristocratic families was of great
importance to Ampleforth. He told Prior Burgess, 'You will
find in Lord Arundell a steady and warm supporter should
this business succeed and the circumstance of your having in
the house at the same time Lord Stourton, an Arundell and
a Clifford is likely to be of greatest service to the College'.[45]
This promotion of the school was not without some success.
By 1830 the Ampleforth school had reached eighty pupils.
This compared to Downside with fewer than forty boys and
around a hundred at Stonyhurst.[46]

It is possible to gain an impression of what the College of
St Laurence was like at the time of Baines. A prospectus for
1815 and a copy of the school rules for 1822 survive, as do
exhibition programmes from 1814 and the course of studies for
1825. Supplementing these are the diary of a pupil from 1815
to 1818, Robert Nihell, and some letters from John Polidori, a
pupil from 1804 to 1810, to his father.

With regard to the curriculum, the July examinations, later
known as exhibitions, were of some importance to Ampleforth.[47] The school's authorities were sensitive to the charge

---

[44]   Edward Clifford, the fifth son of Lord Clifford, became a monk of
       Ampleforth. He had left the school as a layman, but, against his
       father's wishes, returned a few years later to try his vocation. As Fr
       Augustine Clifford he had a rather tumultuous time. In the disputes
       raging around the creation of Prior Park he initially sided with his
       old teacher, Bishop Baines. However, he broke with Baines and made
       a short-lived return to Ampleforth. He finally left in 1831 and ended
       his days in 1841 as a missionary in Mauritius. See Allanson, *English
       Benedictines*, pp. 377–8.

[45]   Ampleforth Abbey Archives, A267 7G39, Letter 6, Baines to Burgess,
       28 February 1820. Fr Laurence Burgess was prior from 1818 to 1830
       when he left Ampleforth to support the by then Bishop Baines's
       scheme for Prior Park. See Cramer, *Ampleforth*, p. 209. For creating
       so much turmoil at Ampleforth, neither Baines nor Burgess were
       given biographies by Allanson.

[46]   The Ampleforth figure is taken from Almond, *Ampleforth*, p. 332;
       Downside from van Zeller, *Downside*, p. 26; and Stonyhurst from
       Muir, *Stonyhurst*, p. 85.

[47]   Ampleforth College still has an exhibition. Today it takes place over
       the last weekend of May and is more of a social occasion, based on

that the breadth of their studies might lead to a lack of depth. Parents and interested parties, therefore, were invited annually to Ampleforth to hear its students publicly examined. As the Prospectus of 1815 said, the examinations were held to dispel the belief that so much could only be covered superficially and to show that the system of learning at Ampleforth was not 'a system of rote calculated to overburden the memory and weaken the judgment'.[48] In the programme for the 1815 examinations is the full text of an address composed by one of the professors and delivered by a student, Edmund Kelly. The burden of this address was that there was much more to the Ampleforth curriculum than the narrow study of the Classics. It is an interesting illustration of how Ampleforth justified and projected its approach to the curriculum.[49]

[48] prize giving, speeches from the headmaster and abbot, a school play and cricket matches against the Old Amplefordians, than an opportunity for the boys to be put through their academic paces. The retention of the name 'exhibition' and the performance of a play, however, represent a link between modern and early Ampleforth. Ampleforth Abbey Archives, EX 01–4.

[49] *Ibid.* The address reads:
Two dreadful languages must first be known
Then blame not us, if trembling we survey
Such frightful ills and tempt another way;
If Athens' sons we mark with envious view,
And strive their footsteps to pursue:
If learning words we sometimes study things;
Sometimes unfetter fancy's airy wings;
On them the wonders of the world explore,
Search every sea and trace out every shore,
Study our nature in th'historic page,
Learn the past the future to presage;
Learn from his glorious works profusely spread,
To worship God with mingled love and dread;
Learn from the bird, the insect and flower,
To bless his goodness, and adore his power:
Ah blame not, if seduc'd by charms so sweet,
We tread a path untrod by other feet.
If aught we lose the lot is not unpaid,
One period of our life is happier made
. . . .
Think not that classic learning we despise,
We own its uses and its charms we prize!

That the College at Ampleforth delivered on its promise to provide more than a narrow classical curriculum can be seen in the examination programmes that follow on from 1815. The core of the Ampleforth curriculum was Greek, history, Latin, geography, French and mathematics. In some years this range was extended by the inclusion of Hebrew, modern languages such as Italian, Spanish and German, and natural history. Hebrew was examined in 1815 with the first class, usually the boys at the top of the school, presenting themselves. Thereafter, Hebrew could be examined by two or three boys being presented, as in 1822 when Cockshoot (a later prior) offered the Book of Judges, and Ryan and Calderbank part of the Book of Job; or more, as in 1817, when three classes were examined in Hebrew.[50] It would seem that subjects outside the core were largely dependent upon the commitment of individual boys to them. In 1820, for example, Arabic made its only appearance at Ampleforth when Gastaldi offered select passages from the Koran.[51] Italian appears to have been quite popular in the 1820s. In 1817 Spanish was on offer when Robert Nihell (the author of a surviving fragment of a diary) was advertised as able to explain some books of Don Quixote. Natural history appears to have peaked in the early years. In 1814, the first class was examined in Linnaeus's order of quadrupeds, fifty-three genera and one-hundred-and-twenty-four species. The second class was examined in ornithology and the first, second and third classes were examined in botany.[52]

There is also an indication that the curriculum could respond to parental demand. In 1815 it was announced that the order in which languages were learned was to be altered: 'At the instigation of the parents who wished their children

O yes, we study Greek and Latin still,
And French and Dutch and Hebrew if you will.
Yes we will study them and learn them too;
But let us then our favourite paths pursue:
Grammars and rods and lexicons remove;
We shudder at them and how can we love?

50 Ampleforth Abbey Archives, EX01-4, 5, 6.
51 Ampleforth Abbey Archives, EX01-6.
52 Ampleforth Abbey Archives, EX01-4.

to learn French as early as possible in order that they may acquire a habit of speaking it with ease and correctness (an object so very important in modern education) it is proposed henceforth to initiate the students in French before they begin the dead languages'. To further the study of French in the College, the French priest, Fr Louis Honore Dehenne, was recruited to the staff.[53]

It would seem from the details given in the examination programme that the studies were not superficial. In every examination programme, details of the books on which pupils were to be examined were given. 1827 can be used as a typical example of what was on offer at Ampleforth in the first third of the nineteenth century. Notwithstanding the insistence that there was more to education than the Classics, Ampleforth boys appear to have made an intensive study of Latin and Greek. The Greek examinations featured Euripides, Sophocles, Homer, Socrates and Xenophon. The Latin examinations were on Horace, Sallust, Virgil, Cicero and Caesar. French studies were based on Massillon, Telemachus and Wanostrocht. History for the senior boys covered from Caesar to the present, while more junior boys studied general history from the Creation until 300 BC, followed by from 300 BC to the end of the Roman Empire. Geography covered delineation and the general geography of the globe. Mathematics for the senior boys dealt with geometry and trigonometry, mensuration, arithmetic and algebra. The second class was taught the principal rules of arithmetic, while the first class had the elementary rules of arithmetic. Drama too featured in the school life of Ampleforth. In the evening of 1827, visitors to the examinations were treated to two plays: *Henry IV, Part One*, and Moliere's *Fourbieres de Scapin*. Dramatic performances were a feature of every exhibition, but for 1827 a separate printed bill giving details of the cast survives. Besides having to take

53 Ampleforth Abbey Archives, EX01, unnumbered document, Examination Programme, 21–2 June 1815. Fr Louis Honore Dehenne is recorded in A. Bellenger, *The French Exiled Clergy in the British Isles after 1789* (Downside: Downside Abbey Books, 1986), p. 171.

a high profile in the examination, senior boys such as Fielding and Darell were also expected to take leading roles in the plays.

It has to be acknowledged that the examination programmes were part of the College's publicity material, and an important part of their purpose was to make the College's range and depth of studies look impressive. At the end of it all, however, the boys had to deliver in public. It would surely have been a risk not worth taking for the College to advertise the expertise of its boys in a range of demanding studies and then have them fail before parents and visitors. To ensure that the boys would not embarrass the College during the July exhibitions, there were regular tests throughout the school year. The school rules of 1822 provided for monthly tests of all classes. Exercises were set by the prefect on the Tuesday and Wednesday immediately before the regular holiday (which fell on the first Thursday of each month).[54] Even after the school was severely affected by defections to Bishop Baines's new project at Prior Park, the exhibitions continued, and there is some evidence that the boys' educational achievements were real and capable of standing up to scrutiny. In 1834 Prior Richard Towers wrote of the success of an exhibition, 'attended by both Catholic secular clergy and by Protestants who took an active part in the examinations and expressed their satisfaction'.[55]

Another feature of Ampleforth revealed by the examination programmes and the 1825 course of studies is evidence of setting by ability. In the programmes the names of boys are frequently given alongside the subjects in which they are to be examined. For a run of programmes in the 1810s there are numbered lists of boys in the College, and the boys presenting in each examination then identified by number. From this it can be seen that boys could be placed in different classes for different subjects. Robert Nihell in 1817, for example, was in the second class for history and the third class for Hebrew.[56]

---

[54] Ampleforth Abbey Archives, BX51–2A, 1822 School Rules, p. 16.
[55] Ampleforth Abbey Archives, DX31 7G14, Item 12, Letter 1, Towers, August 1832.
[56] Ampleforth Abbey Archives, EX01–5.

Something of the quality of academic life at the early Ampleforth can also be seen in the correspondence of John Polidori,
who was later to be the physician of Byron and a minor literary
figure in his own right as the author of *The Vampyr*. Letters
exchanged between Polidori and his father survive from 1806
and 1808–9.[57] Much of this correspondence concerns family
business. In 1808–9, for example, there was an exchange on
the young Polidori's future career. The boy was still prepared
to consider entering the monastic community, an idea he had
mooted in 1806. An uncle had suggested a career in the Indian
Army. In the end, it was decided that John Polidori should
enter the medical profession and when he left Ampleforth in
1810 it was to read medicine at Edinburgh. The letters also give
a glimpse of John Polidori's life at Ampleforth and indicate
that the College was making some progress with the academic
education of its pupil. By the time of his second letter to his
father in 1806 Polidori was able to write part of it in French.
In a later letter, the young Polidori made a request for a dozen
books, including Racine.

Beyond the picture of academic life given by the school's
publicity material, it is possible to gauge something of the
school's life from the other sources. The approach to discipline was laid out in the school rules of 1822, issued under the
authority of Prior Laurence Burgess. Just as Ampleforth inherited the core of its library and school community from Lamspringe, it would also appear indebted to it for its rules. There
are similarities between the 1822 Ampleforth rules and the
surviving rules from Lamspringe, issued by Abbot Maurus
Heatley. In both sets of rules, there is a stress on the integration of the school into the religious life of the monastic community. Particular attention is paid to conduct in church and
there is an emphasis on the Christian principles that should
underpin community life. The Ampleforth rules, however,

---

[57] These letters are kept at the University of British Columbia,
Vancouver. They are used in D. L. MacDonald, *Poor Polidori* (Toronto:
University of Toronto Press, 1988). They have also been used by P.
O'R. Smiley, 'Polidori at Ampleforth', *Ampleforth Journal*, 94 (1989),
pp. 15–25.

can be more concise than those of Lamspringe. For example, 'When the Blessed Sacrament is exposed or be it past the elevation in the Mass at any altar they are to turn towards it, kneel down devoutly and with profound reverence adore the God really present there', becomes in the Ampleforth version 'the greatest attention and reverence should always be paid to the divine presence'.[58]

With regard to the more mundane matters of the ordering school day and discipline, the rules covered rising times (5.45 AM on study days, 6.45 AM on others), deportment at morning Mass, the timing of retreats (the last three days of Holy Week), behaviour towards masters ('Let them the students always consider their masters and superiors as holding the place of God ... and, as such, love and respect them for the care they take of them'), the hours of study (before breakfast, 10 AM to 11.30 AM, 11.50 AM to 12.30 PM, 5.00 PM to 6.15 PM and 8 PM until Night Prayers), disciplinary procedures, monthly examinations, times of silence, regulations for meals, clothing regulations, bounds, dormitory rules, rules for leaving the enclosure and details of school holidays. The principal holidays were the four weeks after the public examination in July and from Christmas to Epiphany. Thereafter, there were day holidays on the first Thursday of every month, the feasts of the Prior, Subprior and Prefect, Shrove Monday and Tuesday, Easter and Whitsun, the feasts of St Thomas of Canterbury, St Benedict Biscop, St Gregory the Great, St George and St Benet, a day for skating 'if the ice bear' and half-days for the feasts of the professors.

This document is far removed from a world in which flogging was the disciplinary staple. Corporal punishment existed at Ampleforth but it came at the end of a quite sophisticated system of disciplinary measures, at the heart of which was the token. Boys were to collect tokens in the five minutes before and after the beginning of study. These tokens were then forfeited for being late, for having dirty shoes or hands, for not

---

58 For the Lamspringe rules, see McClelland, 'School and Studies in Lamspringe', in Cramer, *Lamspringe*, p. 114. For the Ampleforth rules, see Ampleforth Abbey Archives, BX51–2A, pp. 5, 11.

learning lessons, for not having the required books, for being noisy or, in something of a catch-all, for any misbehaviour deemed worthy of the loss of a token by a master. The penalties for the loss of a token were, in the first instance, the loss of a quarter hour's recreation. This was followed by standing during school and, in the third instance, 'depriving the offender of as much recreation as he requires for learning the lesson he has neglected'.[59]

The token system was reinforced by the practice of giving marks. Marks were at a master's discretion when a token had been forfeited and a new offence committed for which a token would be lost. The rules specifically mention breach of silence, neglect of studies and disturbing others. The penalties for those acquiring marks, which were given out every Sunday, Tuesday and Thursday morning, were arranged in a hierarchy. The penalty for the junior boys could range from writing out fair a page of spelling, three lines to be learned by heart from the reading book, one or more sums in arithmetic and analysing half a page from the reading book. The punishment for those in the middle of the school could include ten lines of construing not learned before, learning five lines by heart, analysing a page in English or Latin, marking a plan of a house and measuring a field, building or distance. The oldest boys could be given five verses in Greek or Latin by heart, ten lines to construe, ten lines to be translated into verse or prose or five lines composed on a given subject.[60]

The system in practice may have been some way short of the ideal, as indicated by a handwritten comment on a copy of the school timetable dated August: 'marks neglected, in consequence of which corporal punishments too frequent'. This was followed by the note that it was 'better to stimulate by honor, interest and praise', concluding that 'boys are more easily led than driven'.[61] Nevertheless the discipline in Ampleforth would appear to be some way removed from that obtaining in the contemporary public schools, and certainly the Eton in

[59] Ampleforth Abbey Archives, BX51–2A, p. 11.
[60] Ampleforth Abbey Archives, BX51–2A, p. 14.
[61] Ampleforth Abbey Archives, BX45–06.

which Keate had earned his reputation as a flogger.[62] In the section of the 1822 rules headed 'Corporal Punishment' it was stated that the College's aspiration was that boys would be 'Kept within the bounds of duty by more honourable sentiments than the fear of corporal punishment'. In the section on 'Behaviour to One Another' it was stated that 'Everyone should consider how pleasant and heavenly it is to live in peace and unity together. All beating one another is strictly forbidden.'[63]

The atmosphere of the school and the relationship between staff and pupils is glimpsed in the diary of Robert Nihell. Nihell was at Ampleforth from 1815 to 1818. The diary covers January to June and the days fit the calendar of 1816. The picture that emerges is of boys and staff living together amicably. There is no evidence of the young Nihell feeling oppressed by his scholastic environment. In 1816 it would appear that the rule allowing a recreation day when the ice allowed skating was already in force. In February, Robert Nihell was able record good skating on Fairfax's Pond. The weather and skating prospects were a matter of some interest to the young diarist, but beyond this the diary records the development of the school, the combination of school and pastoral work by the young monks, academic work and the generally good relationship between staff and boys.

The development of the school can be seen in the references to the finishing of a new music school and the completion of a new tailor's room. The finishing of this latter room led to Nihell recording that Mr Rishton treated the workmen to punch to christen the new room. This resulted in everyone 'singing and bawling till twelve o'clock at night. Everyone was drunk'.[64] The school also benefitted from the changing of a stove in the new but damp playroom and the building of the 'ball place' by a Mr Spence. The building of the ball place was of some importance to the early college and represented

---

[62] Dr John Keate, headmaster of Eton, 1808–34. For Keate's belief in flogging (including his flogging of the future prime minister), see P. Magnus, *Gladstone* (London: John Murray, 1970), p. 5.

[63] Ampleforth Abbey Archives, X51–2A, pp. 8–9.

[64] The houses at Ampleforth still have a 'punch' every year to celebrate the house and its patron saint.

another element of continuity with the traditions of the English Catholic schools established in continental exile. These schools developed distinctive games involving the use of racket and ball against walls. Such walls were built quite quickly at both Ampleforth and Stonyhurst.[65]

The work of the community is seen in entries that record monks visiting the sick, and, in March, Fr Laurence going out one evening 'to convert some people at Helmsley and Revis'. The relationship between the community and locality would appear to have been harmonious. On Easter Sunday Nihell recorded that the Chapel was as full as it could be with a large number of Catholics and Protestants. Fr Augustine Baines gave the sermon, which was deemed 'a most excellent sermon all about the Protestants'.[66] The day-to-day life of the school is seen in entries recording events such as Mr Baines examining the boys in their studies from Friday 23 to Saturday 24 of February. Later Mr Baines gave out the places, which the diarist recorded as '1st R. Nihell, R. Allanson, E. Kelly'.[67] There is a record of the boys attending to their gardens (gardens would appear to have been a feature of early Ampleforth life. In one of his letters to his father, John Polidori requested seeds for his garden, along with an order of a dozen crucifixes from a London store for himself and his schoolfellows). The dramatics that were a feature of the College exhibition were also mentioned. In February there were rehearsals and a performance of the (unnamed) play, which resulted in Mr Rishton 'treating the actors with rum and gin biscuits and buns'.

The diary frequently records the boys being taken out for walks by the masters and the general impression is of one of good nature between staff and pupils. There is an implicit criticism of the staff in the record that 'they would not let us

[65] Muir, *Stonyhurst*, p. 80. The great hard ball wall was built in 1796, just two years after the school's foundation at Stonyhurst.

[66] Ampleforth Abbey Archives, Nihell Diary.

[67] Robert Allanson was the elder brother of Peter Allanson, later Fr Athanasius Allanson, monk of St Laurence's and biographer of the English Benedictines. Peter was at school at this time, having joined as an eight-year-old. See introduction to Allanson, *English Benedictines*, p. vii.

have play' on the Feast of St Gregory (under the 1822 rules this would have been a recreation day), but there are more records of play being allowed on the feast days of the masters, and incidents such as that of Tuesday 4 June, when

> Anselm and Jerome take the boys to Byland and in the afternoon Placid took us to Oswaldkirk Wood. Some of us made a swing there. When we came home we had the tea and punch which Anselm had promised.

Similarly, in May there had been an occasion when

> Bede left us to go upon the Mission near Wigan. We had play for him and in the morning the boys went to Byland and in the afternoon we had dancing for which Mr Burgess forgave us our marks.[68]

The celebration of a monk leaving Ampleforth to go out on missionary work in the parishes of Lancashire and Yorkshire, the responsibility of the community of St Laurence since its Dieulouard days, is of interest in understanding how the school operated.[69] The school at this time, indeed throughout the nineteenth century, was an enterprise conducted principally by young monks. The focus of the community was on its parishes. Once ordained, monks would usually be sent out 'on the missions'. The boys in the school were taught by young monks who themselves were undergoing teaching. Obviously, it does not follow that young teachers have to be more sympathetic to their charges or less severe than older men. There was a requirement for formality at Ampleforth. Just as at Lamspringe, the Ampleforth rules required boys to bow when encountering monks. The youthfulness of its teaching staff, however, is something that distinguished a monastic school from other English schools where schoolmastering

---

[68] Ampleforth Abbey Archives, Nihell Diary.
[69] A list of Ampleforth parishes is given in Cramer, *Ampleforth*, p. 211. The mission parishes run by Ampleforth monks in this period were: Aberford, Leeds (1793), Brownedge, Preston (1780), Brandsby, Yorkshire (1791), Brindle, Preston (1786), Easingwold, Yorkshire (1794), Knaresborough, Yorkshire (1693), St Peter's, Liverpool (1788), St Alban's, Warrington (1771), Warwick Bridge, Carlisle (1720) and Workington, Cumbria (1810).

was a career. The impression given in the Nihell diary is that the young monks of Ampleforth were not especially severe as teachers. The picture of the relationship between boys and masters drawn from Nihell's writings is one far removed from that prevalent in the great Anglican schools, where, in Mangan's view, 'before 1850 ... the public school master was a distant figure to his boys and for the most part indifferent to their extra-curricular pastimes'.[70]

The Ampleforth of the first third of the nineteenth century, therefore, would appear to have been a successful school. It was not, however, able to enjoy a period of uninterrupted success, and, ironically, the author of its misfortunes was Fr Augustine Baines, the man responsible for so much of its progress. Baines's energy and willingness to innovate in education led him to look beyond the confines of the school at Ampleforth. As Coadjutor of the Western Province, Baines began formulating plans for the improvement of Catholic education in the district as early as 1823. When he succeeded as bishop, he pursued his plan in earnest. His vision was to establish an educational centre at Prior Park, near Bath. Prior Park would accommodate a seminary, a school for the sons of the gentry and a centre for higher studies that would, in effect, become a Catholic university.[71]

This scheme had damaging consequences for the existing schools at Downside and Ampleforth. Baines originally planned to use the monastic community at Downside to staff his establishment. The Downside community, however, was reluctant to be drawn into the scheme. In the course of his dispute with the Downside monks, and determined to bring them under his episcopal authority, Baines challenged the validity of the monastic orders of the English Benedictine Congregation.[72] Unsuccessful in Somerset, he turned to his

---

[70] Mangan, *Athleticism*, p. 113.
[71] For details of Baines's plans, see J. S. Roche, *A History of Prior Park and its Founder, Bishop Baines* (London: Burns and Oates, 1931) and Gilbert, *This Restless Prelate*, pp. 48–57.
[72] For Baines's views that English Benedictines were not monks but secular priests subject to the jurisdiction of bishops, see Gilbert, *This Restless Prelate*, p. 79.

former brethren in Yorkshire. He had been considering using the community of St Laurence from the outset of his thinking about the improvement of educational provision in the Western District. In 1823 he had written to Prior Burgess, 'It is impossible to describe to you what a pleasure it would be to me to have Ampleforth in the west ... But alas! I fear that we shall meet with great obstruction and difficulty from some of your brethren.' In 1830, Baines travelled to Yorkshire and very nearly overcame the resistance he had foreseen seven years earlier.[73] He had the support of Prior Burgess and after discussions with the community was able to persuade the novices and some monks, notably Metcalf, Rooker, Clifford and Glover, of the rightness of his plan. He was not, however, able to maintain the support of all. When it came to the actual destruction of the Ampleforth community, and the ruthlessness with which Baines was prepared to pursue this became apparent, Clifford and Glover turned against him. Edward Glover had been one of the party that had arrived in England with him in 1803. While Baines might have been prepared to see Ampleforth transferred as a school, much as his own school at Lamspringe had been, in the end Glover was not. He wrote to Prior Burgess that 'As his [Baines's] plans have become known they seem totally subversive of the Benedictine order in England ... history will record that he gave the blow and, as he has struck at Downside, he has ruined Ampleforth, at which we have been labouring these years and raised it to some degree of eminence'.[74] Clifford's break with Baines was reported by Fr Joseph Brown of Downside. In a letter to the Benedictine Provincial, Fr James Deday, he wrote 'Clifford is now red hot with rage against Baines and co. He has gone round to the parents at Liverpool of children at Ampleforth and exposed the system of Baines and co.'[75]

---

[73] The ability of Bishop Baines to sway the Ampleforth community is attested by records left by Fr Augustine Lowe and Caldwell. Ampleforth Abbey Archives, A268. Gilbert, *This Restless Prelate*, p. 84.

[74] Clifton Diocesan Archives, Baines Box File 4, Glover to Burgess, 9 February 1830. Gilbert, *This Restless Prelate*, p. 84.

[75] Downside Archives, H59, Brown to Deday, 27 May 1830. Gilbert, *This Restless Prelate*, p. 90.

In the end, Ampleforth was not ruined. Just the three priests (Burgess, Rooker and Metcalf) left the community, along with a couple of novices.[76] While, in the view of one of its early historians, 'the cream of the school, some thirty boys, most of them of distinguished families',[77] left for Prior Park in 1830, the school at Ampleforth was able to survive. In the 1831 exhibition programme, when the College was reduced to thirty-one, its plight was apparent, but equally there was a resolve to carry on. This can be seen in the concluding note of the new prior, Fr Richard Towers:

> Parents who are immediately concerned with the students are particularly requested to hono[u]r the existing exhibition with their presence in order to form their own unbiased judgment of the progress made by the students during the last year, which the public well knows has been a year of peculiar and extraordinary difficulties for the establishment. We feel conscious that parents, taking into consideration the obstacles that have been surmounted, will not only find reason to be satisfied with the attainments of the last year, but will also from thence receive a pledge of the success, with which we flatter ourselves, the exertions of the ensuing year will be crowned when freed from many incumbrances [sic] of the last.
>
> We are the more earnest in pressing the above request, as many reports have been incessantly circulated, tending to bring this establishment into disrepute, and even to impress upon the Public mind, the unfounded

[76] The novices at the time were Peter Hutton, Moses Furlong, Thomas Swale and Gregory Flinn. According to Ampleforth tradition, Flinn would have nothing to do with Baines from the outset, while the others were persuaded. In the end, Hutton and Furlong followed Baines with Hutton eventually becoming the first President of the Rosminian foundation, Ratcliffe College. See Cramer, *Ampleforth*, p. 70.

[77] Almond, *Ampleforth*, p. 320. The opening of a school at Prior Park also harmed the numbers at Downside. In 1830 Downside had 62 pupils. In the 1830s the numbers were in the thirties. See van Zeller, *Downside*, p. 40.

idea that this College has been for some time past on
the eve of total dissolution.[78]

In the end, Bishop Baines's grand design did not come to fruition. His challenge to the validity of the monastic vows taken
by those in opposition to him failed.[79] The school at Prior Park,
after initial success, fared badly and was then ruined by a fire.
The school kept going after this, but it was never again in a
position to challenge Ampleforth or Downside. The plan for
a seminary and centre for higher studies was even less successful. By 1857, Baines's centre for higher studies, St Paul's,
had closed. Baines was not able to persuade other bishops
to abandon their own seminaries and was unable to secure
important lay patronage. Baines was not supported by influential lay Catholics. He was opposed by Pugin, who resented
Baines's dislike of the Gothic, and Lord Shrewsbury. Other
English Catholic bishops disliked his connections with the
Irish hierarchy. Baines was briefly able to attract Fr Nicholas
Wiseman to his centre for higher studies in 1835, but in the
end Wiseman, and his prestige, transferred to the seminary
of the Midlands diocese, Oscott.[80]

By the 1830s, therefore, Ampleforth had been, to a large
extent, made and almost destroyed by the mercurial talents
of Fr Augustine Baines. In the years after 1830 the school gave
up its commitment to Feinaigle's method of memory training
and became more conventional in its approach to teaching. It
lost its gentry pupils and recruited largely from its parishes in
Lancashire and Yorkshire. Some boys joined the community,
others returned to middle-class lives. In the words of one of
Ampleforth's most distinguished modern old boys, Sir David
Goodall, 'The typical 19th century Amplefordian came from a

[78] Ampleforth Abbey Archives, EX01 7, Exhibition Programme, July
      1831.
[79] Fr Joseph Brown of Downside and the first prior of Ampleforth, Fr
      Richard Marsh, were able to put the case for the English Benedictines
      successfully in Rome. See Gilbert, *Restless Prelate*, p. 86.
[80] See V. A. McClelland, *English Roman Catholics and Higher Education*
      (Oxford: Clarendon Press, 1973), pp. 9–12.

relatively modest, middle class family, probably in the north of England. Often he would have relations among the monks.'[81]

An illustration of the extent to which Ampleforth ceased to operate amongst the families of the Catholic elite can be seen in the number of its Irish pupils. Recent research has shown that the Irish Catholic gentry from 1850 shunned the elite schools of the Anglican establishment and, notwithstanding the existence in Ireland of Catholic schools comparable to those in England, sent their children abroad for their education, mostly to England but also France and Belgium.[82] In England, the Irish Catholic gentry, looking for those schools with the greatest prestige, sent their sons, for the most part, to Stonyhurst, Downside, Beaumont and Oscott. Between 1850 and 1900 the numbers of Irish boys in these schools were: Stonyhurst 462, Downside 309, Beaumont 294, and Oscott 238. Downside averaged 36 per cent of its intake from Ireland throughout the 1870s, 50 per cent in some years.[83] At Ampleforth, however, between 1802 and 1895, only 81 of the 1634 boys educated there were Irish born, approximately 5 per cent of the intake.[84]

While Ampleforth, therefore, was settling down as one of several schools serving the English Catholic community in the mid-nineteenth century, and with a distinctively Catholic approach to education, the wider world of secondary educa-

---

[81] Sir David Goodall, 'Ampleforth Alumni', in A. Marett-Crosby (ed.), *A School of the Lord's Service, A History of Ampleforth College* (London: James and James, 2002), p. 126.

[82] C. O'Neill, *Catholics of Consequence-Transnational Education, Social Mobility and the Irish Catholic Elite, 1850–1900* (Oxford: Oxford University Press, 2014). In O'Neill's view, 'For Irish families a nineteenth-century boarding school education in Britain or on the Continent remained an important signifier of elite status and in fact provided something equivalent to the eighteenth century "Grand Tour"'. *Ibid.*, p. 4. The Irish Catholic boarding schools comparable to those in England were Clongowes Wood College, Kildare, and St Stanilaus College, Offaly (both Jesuit), Castlenock, Dublin (Vincentian) and Blackrock College, Dublin (Holy Ghost Fathers). *Ibid.*, p. 12.

[83] *Ibid.*, p. 69.

[84] Marett-Crosby, *Ampleforth*, p. 127.

tion saw the creation of the English public school. From the perspective of middle class and gentry education for British Catholics, the relationship of schools such as Ampleforth to these public schools was to become crucial in determining their place in British society.

4

Ampleforth and the Catholic Schools in the Victorian Period

I
N THE 1830S, Ampleforth and the other Catholic schools existed outside of the world of the Anglican public schools. Towards the end of the nineteenth century, Stonyhurst and, to a lesser extent Downside, moved closer to its fringes. As Bamford has commented on the Catholic and Nonconformist schools founded at the start of the nineteenth century:

> All these non-Anglican ventures, of whatever denomination, were classical boarding schools, in part at least, but were small and negligible in the number of boys they dealt with. In no real or competitive sense were they comparable at this stage to the hard core of Anglican schools.[1]

In this period, the Catholic schools built on the educational traditions established on the continent. Where they engaged in educational innovation, it was in a manner distinct from developments in the larger Anglican schools.

For much of Victoria's reign there was a possibility (albeit a faint one, as events proved) that Catholic schools would remain part of a separate educational tradition and that Catholic education for the middle and upper classes would not be assimilated into the wider educational world: a world dominated by the public schools and the universities of Oxford and Cambridge. By 1895, however, and with the decision of Rome that Catholics were no longer prohibited by the Church from

---

[1] Bamford, *The Rise of the Public Schools*, p. xiv.

attending Oxford and Cambridge,[2] the prospect of Catholic education to university level remaining isolated from the mainstream was extinguished.

It was from this time that the English Catholic public school genuinely emerged, as Catholic schools organized themselves to prepare their pupils for university education at Oxford and Cambridge. H. O. Evennett, a beneficiary of the change and old boy of Downside and Fellow of Trinity College, Cambridge, commented upon the extent to which some Catholic schools were shaped by the opportunity to prepare their boys for admission to Oxford and Cambridge.[3] In his history of Catholic education in England, he remarked of the Church's rescinding of its ban on Catholics attending Oxford and Cambridge, 'This factor, so powerful in determining the scope and methods of school courses did much to approximate the courses of study in Catholic schools to those of the Public Schools and grammar schools still more closely'.[4]

It was in this period that Ampleforth came into its own as a public school. Catholic schools, which had eclipsed Ampleforth for much of the nineteenth century, either did not become involved in the attempt to create English Catholic public schools or became less successful competitors. However, before looking in detail at the development of Ampleforth from 1895, it is necessary to examine the nineteenth-century background to the integration of Catholic education into the wider national picture.

Coming into the Victorian period, stemming from traditions developed during the time of continental exile, the Catholic secondary schools for boys differed from the schools that were to dominate the public school world (the schools of the Clarendon Commission), in their curriculum, their teaching methods, their pastoral provisions and social composition. Much of the distinctiveness of the Catholic schools' curricular provisions derived from their social composition. The Catholic schools,

---

2   See McClelland, *English Roman Catholics*, p. 384.
3   van Zeller, *Downside*, p. 116. Evennett was elected a Fellow of Trinity College in 1926.
4   Evennett, *The Catholic Schools*, p. 100

while they always had a section of the English gentry and aristocracy to educate, were not gentry-dominated schools. Catholic gentry families could bring patronage and prestige to schools, but their numbers were not large in the mid-nineteenth century and their support could be fickle. Ampleforth at the time of Baines might be the place supported by the aristocracy and gentry. Later it would be Wiseman's Oscott, and, for brief spells, Newman's Oratory or Petre's Woburn.[5] Catholic schools, if they were to survive long term, could not gear themselves exclusively to the gentry. For the most part, they had to look to the middle classes. Catholic priests, moreover, tended to come from the middle ranks of society. The lay boys who were educated alongside the prospective priests at Sedgley Park, Oscott, Ushaw and the rest were also from this social background. The existence of a core of middle-class boys, to a large extent, determined the curriculum.

The position in the public schools was a little different. They too were essentially middle-class schools, but schools for which a curriculum based on the Classics was appropriate. As the empirical research of Rubenstein, in his study of the relationship between the culture of Britain's elite and the economy in the industrial age has shown, the aristocracy and gentry were educated at Eton and the leading schools, but, even in these, and overwhelmingly elsewhere, the English public schools were dominated by the professional middle classes. According to Rubenstein, 'it is hardly an exaggeration to say that the nineteenth-century public schools were schools for the sons of the professional middle classes'.[6] Schools catering for the sons of Anglican clergymen, civil servants, lawyers, military and naval men could afford to have a curriculum

[5] See V. A. McClelland, 'School or Cloister? An English Educational Dilemma, 1794–1889', *Paedagogica Historica*, 20/1 (1980), pp. 108–28.
[6] W. D. Rubenstein, *Capitalism, Culture and Decline in Britain, 1750–1990* (London: Routledge, 1993), p. 119. See pp. 105–39 for a detailed discussion of the social composition of English public schools. A similar point about the domination of the public schools by professional families, especially those founded in the nineteenth century, can be found in F. M. L Thompson, *The Rise of Respectable Society* (London: Fontana Press, 1988), p. 66.

dominated by the teaching of Greek and Latin. This was not the case in the Catholic colleges and schools.

While the Classics were an important part of the curriculum offered in the various Catholic schools and colleges, the need to cater for boys from those sections of the middle class whose incomes derived from business meant that there was always a pressure to offer something more. This can be seen in examples drawn from a variety of schools. At Stonyhurst, the prefect of studies in 1814, Fr Charles Brookes, was determined that there should be some breadth in the curriculum. He wrote that 'On looking at our list of scholars, it appears that the greater part of them are to be employed when they leave the college in some sort of mercantile business. To all of these arithmetic is the science which will be most useful and interesting.'[7] Early on, therefore, Stonyhurst had a classroom dedicated to mathematics. In 1824 this was joined by a chemistry laboratory.[8] The revised Ratio Studiorum, issued to Jesuit colleges in 1832, reinforced curricular breadth at Stonyhurst. Provincials were required to promote the study of vernacular languages, history, geography and the sciences.

At Ushaw an advertisement in the *Catholic Directory* for 1834 stated that for £50 per annum scholars would be offered Latin and Greek and English, French, book keeping, writing, arithmetic, history and geography.[9] At Sedgley Park, and later Cotton College, the curriculum was clearly designed to cater for middle-class boys who had to make their way in the world. The nineteenth-century historian of Sedgley Park, Fr Husenbeth, commented of the school's curriculum, 'A good commercial education was its principal aim and object; ever subordinate, however, to the sound and careful inculcation of religious knowledge and practical piety'.[10] He went on to say, 'In a school founded for boys in middle life, mostly destined for commerce, it was not usual for many to learn French and

[7]   Quoted in Muir, *Stonyhurst*, p. 81.
[8]   *Ibid.*
[9]   Milburn, *Ushaw*, p. 138.
[10] Husenbeth, *Sedgley Park*, p. 27.

fewer still learned Latin or Greek'.[11] Latin and Greek were principally for the boys intended for the priesthood.

Teaching methods, derived from continental practice, were also distinctive. Boys between nine and sixteen were usually taught by young clerics. They could be taught in separate classrooms by subject masters at a time when the practice in the great Anglican schools was to have all forms in a common school room being drilled in the Classics. At Sedgley Park in the 1810s, Husenbeth recorded that there were six studies each under its own master and that separate masters taught French, Latin and Greek.[12]

The level of supervision provided for Catholic schoolboys also remained different. As the earlier discussion of what made a Victorian public school has shown, central to the public school tradition was the delegation of responsibility to prefects and the supervision of younger boys by those more senior. Outside of the schoolroom, the Victorian public school master had little contact with his pupils or responsibility for supervising their behaviour. This was not the case in the Catholic Schools with their prefects of discipline and regular supervision of boys outside of formal lessons. During the Taunton Commission, Stonyhurst was visited by James Bryce in 1865. In his report he commented, 'The most peculiar feature in the disciplinary system is the superintendence so unremittingly maintained at all hours'.[13] At Sedgley Park, 'When the boys went into their studies they were all thrown open, so that the watch master perambulated them to preserve order until each master came into his study',[14] and 'In playtime boys were always under the care of one of the masters'.[15] Ushaw extended the practice of supervision, and contact between boys and teachers, with its system of pedagogues. These were young clerics at the head of the college who supervised the academic progress of small groups of four or so boys.[16] This degree of supervision did

[11]   *Ibid.*, p. 87.
[12]   *Ibid.*, p. 92.
[13]   Muir, *Stonyhurst*, p. 98.
[14]   Husenbeth, *Sedgley Park*, p. 92.
[15]   *Ibid.*, p. 108.
[16]   Milburn, *Ushaw*, pp. 139–40.

not have to be oppressive. Arguably, the Catholic schools of the mid-Victorian period were spared many of the problems associated with the boy-based disciplinary systems of the public schools. In a study of Oscott, McClelland has commented:

> The college enjoyed, too, an enviable reputation as an institution where relationships between masters and pupils were easy and unrestrained and where teachers shared the games and amusements of the boys. Amherst recorded 'there was little or no bullying of small boys by bigger ones' and pointed out that 'the fagging system, common to all the Protestant public schools was utterly unknown'. The lay boys destined for professional life were treated with 'openness and frankness'.[17]

As has been remarked earlier, however, the whole issue of the continued development of a separate Catholic tradition in secondary education was conditional upon the university question. McClelland has shown how the Catholic Church in England came to abandon attempts to remain aloof from the higher education endorsed by the English state.[18] For the purposes of this study, however, it is useful to look at why there was so much opposition for so long to the integration of Catholics into the English university system and the repercussions of this for Catholic schools.

The objection to Catholics to attending Anglican universities was that Catholic youth would be exposed to the twin dangers of Protestantism and secularism. For Cardinal Manning, and those who supported him in maintaining the bar on Catholics at Oxford and Cambridge, the ancient universities could not win. On one level, they were objectionable because of their Anglicanism. Catholics taught by Anglicans and surrounded by Anglican fellow students might have their faith weakened. On the other hand, as the century progressed, Oxford and Cambridge were deemed too worldly. Protestant academics were not making an adequate stand against the seculariz-

---

[17] V. A. McClelland, 'Tractarian Intellectualism and the Silent Heritage, 1840–50', in J. F. Champ (ed.), *Oscott College, 1838–1988, A Volume of Commemorative Essays* (Oscott: Oscott Publishing, 1988), p. 88.
[18] McClelland, *English Roman Catholics*.

ing forces of the second half of the nineteenth century. The involvement of Anglican clergymen, most of them with Oxford connections, in the publication of *Essays and Reviews* in 1860 with its agenda for the re-thinking of Christianity in the light of modern scholarship, was a case in point.[19] Catholic students would only be safe in the world of higher education if that world were a Catholic one.

Such attitudes can be seen in the responses of James Spencer Northcote and Cardinal Manning to the idea that Catholics might study at Oxford and Cambridge. When in 1854 Oxford and Cambridge Universities lifted their own restrictions on the admission of Catholics, James Spencer Northcote argued in *The Rambler* that

> For ourselves, however, we most heartily trust that no Catholics will be found to avail themselves of the permission thus accorded. It would be a most pernicious thing for any young Catholic to receive his education at Protestant hands, whether those hands were High Church, Low Church, Latitudinarian, Nonconformist, or Infidel. Education can no more be dissevered from religion than matter from its properties of form and colour ... We therefore trust that, notwithstanding the 'opening' made for us by acts of the legislature or the English Universities themselves, our gentry and aristocracy will hold themselves aloof from the seducing bait and will prefer the advantages of Catholic learning and the honours of a Catholic seminary to that fictitious knowledge and tarnished reputation which are all that Oxford and Cambridge could confer on us.[20]

Regarding the secularizing influences at Oxford and Cambridge, Cardinal Manning's view was expressed in *The Dublin Review* of 1863:

> What we most fear is that Catholics may cast themselves willingly, or be drawn unconsciously, into the stream which is evidently carrying English society every year

---

[19] See *ibid.*, pp. 181–3, for a discussion of the impact of *Essays and Reviews* on Catholic opinion.

[20] *Ibid.*, p. 179.

more and more decidedly and perceptibly towards worldliness and Rationalism.[21]

There were, however, prospects for the creation of a safe higher educational environment for Catholics. The ideal was the establishment of an English Catholic university. This had been the hope of Baines for Prior Park. Cardinal Manning tried to create a Catholic university in Kensington.[22] Beyond the foundation of a Catholic university, however, there was always the option of developing Catholic higher education within the established Catholic colleges. The non-denominational University of London gave the possibility of degrees that could be studied for at Stonyhurst, Oscott, Ushaw and Ware. Catholic higher education could have developed in the nineteenth century with the pinnacle of the system being the university at Kensington or degree study, for clerics and laymen, at one of the existing colleges. Just as Bishop Baines had intended his Catholic university to be fed by a school, so Cardinal Manning opened schools in London. In 1863, St Charles College was founded, directed by Manning's nephew William. Modelled on the public school system, it tended to attract the sons of the professional middle classes. In 1873 the rector of Manning's University College, Thomas Capel, opened Kensington Catholic Public School to cater exclusively for the sons of gentlemen. Just as, however, Baines's plans for Catholic education had foundered on over-ambition, personality clashes and poor administration, so too did Manning's in London. The Kensington school and university had closed by the century's end.[23]

Had Manning been successful, Catholic secondary education might have maintained its distinctive traditions and developed new approaches that were specific to the demands of the community from which its students were drawn. There would have been no need to turn some, at least, of the Catholic schools into institutions, modelled on the English public schools, pre-

---

[21]   *Ibid.*, p. 183.
[22]   *Ibid.*, p. 331. The Catholic University College existed at Cromwell Place, South Kensington, from 1878 to 1882.
[23]   For the Kensington School, see Shrimpton, *Catholic Eton*, p. 250.

paring boys for admission to Oxford and Cambridge. Indeed, throughout the debates on the issue of Catholics and higher education, instances of an alternative Catholic educational vision appear.

An example of this is provided by discussion of the curriculum. In his study of Cardinal Manning's involvement in educational issues, McClelland pointed out that Manning wanted Catholic education to embrace a broader range of studies than the narrow Classicism dictated by Oxford and Cambridge:

> Much of his educational policy as Archbishop can be attributed to his urgent desire to wean the Roman Catholic laity away from the traditional and classical branch of studies, as prescribed at Oxford and Cambridge and advocated by the Jesuits and Newman, towards the scientific and modern branch, and thus he hoped to achieve a reconciliation between the claims of science and those of the Church.[24]

Besides making changes in educational practice, old traditions could have been preserved. The education of lay boys alongside intending priests, which Oakeley defended on the grounds that it prevented 'the entire secularization of the layman',[25] might have been maintained.

At the most fundamental level, there was, arguably, a distinctive Catholic approach to the whole notion of what constituted an education. This contrast in thinking between Catholics and the Anglican establishment was picked up by the convert, Frederick Oakeley. Oakeley had had a distinguished academic career at Balliol and Christ Church. Writing in *The Rambler* in 1848, Oakeley observed of the current debates within Catholic circles about education that

> The difference between the existing English Catholic idea of education and that to which we (converts) were accustomed at Oxford is, as you know, a fundamental one, the one making the formation of (mental) character

---

[24] V. A. McClelland, *Cardinal Manning, His Public Life and Influence 1865–1892* (Oxford: Oxford University Press, 1962), pp. 13–14.

[25] *The Rambler*, 11 December 1848, quoted by McClelland in Champ, *Oscott*, p. 90.

its great aim, the other, the storing of the mind with a certain amount of valuable facts. Hence our requirements seem to Catholics 'limited' and their intellectual character and habits seem to us shallow and desultory.[26]

As Mack observed of the developments in the public school world of the 1870s,

> To the Catholics no amount of reform could make the essentially worldly public schools, with their doctrines of freedom, conform to Catholic ideals of Christian teaching to be achieved by careful and constant supervision. To the *Dublin Review* 'the public school system, as Dean Stanley says, is distinguished — and as we confidently add, distinguished for the worse — from almost every other system of education in Europe'.[27]

Even on the eve of the decision coming from Rome that Catholics could attend Oxford and Cambridge, there were still English Catholic bishops who regretted this development and its likely consequences. Bishop Gordon of Leeds and Bishop Wilkinson of Hexham commented on the petition, 'Fancy our colleges being turned into preparatory schools for these heretic and infidel making shops'. Gordon went on to respond to a proposal that funding should be found for a Catholic professorship at Oxford: 'We want money for the poor schools and we can't be called upon to give money to help aristocrats and snobs on the High Road to Hell'.[28]

The option, however, of maintaining a distinctive Catholic approach to education, with the goal of a Catholic university, was not taken. It is easy enough, certainly with the benefit of hindsight, to see why this would be the case. The social and educational forces working for the integration of Catholic education into the national picture were more powerful than those working for the maintenance of a separate tradition.

---

[26]   McClelland, *English Roman Catholics*, p. 65.
[27]   Reference to *Dublin Review*, October 1878, p. 288, quoted in E. C. Mack, *Public Schools and British Public Opinion*, vol. II (New York: Greenfield Publishing Group, 1941), p. 160.
[28]   McClelland, *English Roman Catholics*, p. 383.

With regard to the relative standards of learning in the Catholic colleges and the Anglican public schools, Catholic opinion eventually swung to the view that what was offered by the Anglican educational world was superior. In the 1840s, Bishop Ullathorne and others might have been able to defend what was offered in Catholic colleges against converts who attacked their academic standards. Stung by criticism of Anglican converts, notably W. G. Ward, Ullathorne wrote, 'We have seen ourselves set forth as the worst taught, worst trained and most ignorant men of our class in all of England'.[29] He went on to draw on his own experience of education at Downside in the 1820s, where he had learnt Greek, Latin, French, Italian, English, history, geography, arithmetic and mathematics. English had included the study of Shakespeare and 'the principal of Classics was studied downright ... and more than once, as boys, we were amused at seeing new companions from Protestant schools, who boasted their upper classes, put down to Caesar to learn their rudiments'.[30] By the latter part of the nineteenth century, however, the more prevalent view seems to have been that of another convert, T. W. Allies, who was recorded as saying 'He had never met with an individual Catholic priest or layman who did not think and feel that English Catholics in the matter of education were far inferior to their Protestant countrymen'.[31]

Further evidence for a lack of Catholic confidence in what they were doing can be seen in the Jesuit refusal to accept much credit for the standards achieved by their pupils in examinations of the University of London. A good illustration of this was provided by an exchange during the collection of evidence on secondary schools by the Taunton Commission. Lord Lyttleton put it to Fr Kingdon, the Prefect of Studies at Stonyhurst, 'We have evidence with regard to the Matriculation Examination of the London University, that your boys come up better prepared than perhaps any school in England

---

[29] Letter to *The Tablet*, 9 December 1848. Cited in McClelland, 'School or Cloister?', p. 119.
[30] *Ibid.*, p. 125.
[31] *Ibid.*, p. 114.

with regard to Classics'. The response of Fr Kingdon was 'I should not myself lay great stress on that fact because you are no doubt aware that the first public schools of the country do not send their candidates to the London University; ... therefore it is not a competition against the whole of England, but is mainly against second-class schools'.[32]

Similarly, in 1871 a bishops' sub-committee on Catholic higher education reported, 'We do not come near Eton, Rugby, Cheltenham, Wellington and some other non-Catholic schools in three respects, viz. first in scholarship; secondly and much more in composition, some varieties of which, for instance Greek verse, are entirely unknown amongst us; thirdly an expansion of mind, earnestness of purpose, definiteness of aim'.[33] Twenty-five years on at the Conference of Catholic Colleges, Archbishop Vaughan referred to an article by Henry. W. New that argued 'Catholic young men of eighteen and nineteen are not intellectually equal to, or as well educated as those who have been brought up in the Public Schools'.[34]

Of some interest in this breast-beating within the Catholic elite when comparing its schools and their Anglican counterparts is the propensity of Catholic commentators to ignore the extent to which the Anglican public schools during the nineteenth century had adopted structures and practices that had been commonplace within the Catholic educational tradition. While the house system and prefects with disciplinary powers were foreign to the Catholic tradition, regulated days, tight discipline, a varied curriculum and subjects taught in separate classrooms were not. In Joyce's study of the part played the public schools in the formation of the ruling class of the British state, he remarks, 'what has been almost entirely left out of public school literature is serious theoretical reflection on the spatial and temporal reorganization of the daily routine of

32 McClelland, *English Roman Catholics*, pp. 43–4.
33 G. A. Beck (ed.), *English Catholics, 1850–1950* (London: Burns and Oates, 1950). Cited in Ampleforth Abbey Archives, NX57 7M 12, unpublished biography of Fr Paul Nevill by Fr Columba Cary-Elwes, version 3, p. 22.
34 *Ibid*. The quotation from H. W. New appears in *The Downside Review*, 1897, p. 184.

the school'. In addressing this, he draws upon the theories of Foucault regarding the role of education in the development of a disciplined society, concluding that 'As an institution the English public school was more Foucauldian than Foucault'.[35] To sustain this, he looks at public school routine as it had developed by the 1870s, focusing on schools' disciplinary codes and their use of time and of space; especially the development of detailed timetables, sets of rules and the shift from common schoolrooms to individual classrooms. He also highlights the use of examinations to produce rank orders for pupils.[36] Much of this may have been new to schools such as Eton, Rugby, Winchester *et al.*, but would have been familiar to schoolboys in the Catholic schools in continental exile in the seventeenth and eighteenth centuries or in nineteenth-century Stonyhurst, Downside and Ampleforth.[37]

Notwithstanding this, however, the predominant view within the Catholic elite was that its leading schools were deficient and change had to be made in the direction of emulating the practice of the leading Anglican schools. This willingness to integrate within the educational provision of the wider society can be seen at all levels. When it came to the education of the Catholic poor, while the Church wished to maintain as much control as possible over the education of its

[35] Joyce, *The State of Freedom*, p. 270. For Foucault's theories, see M. Foucault, *Discipline and Punish* (London: Penguin, 1979). Foucault was principally concerned with the treatment of criminals and the history of the prison. He saw similarities, however, in the ways that surveillance and supervision were developed from the eighteenth century in prisons, factories and schools. See Foucault, *Discipline*, pp. 175–6. Foucault's theories have been of great interest to educational writers, although as Stephen J. Ball has acknowledged, 'what Foucault had to say about education ... was not much'. Stephen J. Ball, *Foucault, Power and Education* (Abingdon: Routledge, 2013), p. 26.

[36] Joyce, *State of Freedom*, pp. 270–6. For school routine and the monitoring of pupils in the 1870s, see: R. Lambert, *The Hothouse Society: An Exploration of Boarding School Life through the Boys' and Girls' Own Writing* (London: Littlehampton Book Services, 1968), pp. 96–105.

[37] See Chapters 2 and 3 for the use of individual classrooms, regulated days and classification by examination in Catholic schools.

young people, the Church needed state money and ran its voluntary schools within the structure of the state system. In the matter of building up and educating a Catholic middle class, again, the Church could not stay aloof from the wider society. Schools such as St Bede's in Manchester were established for this purpose, and the boys produced by such schools were allowed to attend the provincial universities established in the second half of the nineteenth century. The continued bar on the Catholic aristocracy and gentry attending the ancient universities in these circumstances seemed increasingly perverse. Why should upper-class Catholics be cut off from the best available, or most appropriate, education when this was not the case elsewhere?

Besides the triumph of the Anglican educational ideal, based on the public schools and the Oxford and Cambridge colleges, the other significant developments determining the future of secondary education for the Catholic upper middle class and gentry, and which were to be of considerable importance in the rise of Ampleforth, were failed nineteenth-century attempts to create Catholic schools that emulated the Anglican public schools and the change in character of the diocesan colleges educating church and lay students. By the century's end, Oscott (completely) and Ushaw (effectively) had abandoned the teaching of lay students and were seminaries. Before this change, Ushaw and Oscott, especially the latter, were colleges that educated many of the sons of the Catholic gentry. Coming into the twentieth century, schools and colleges that might have been powerful rivals to Ampleforth in the business of becoming Catholic schools in the public school mode, and which might have attracted the Catholic social elite, had already changed direction.

The background to these developments derived in part from disputes at the start of the century about the best means of educating the Catholic aristocracy and gentry. As McClelland has shown, for much of the nineteenth century there was a strained relationship between the old English Catholic gentry and the bishops of the English Church. This strained relationship covered a wide range of issues from how the Church was organized in England to the style of Catholic religious practice. The Catholic gentry tended to hanker after a world in which they were the dominant force in English Catholicism. Nineteenth-century English Catholicism, however, had less to do with ancient Catholic families keeping the faith alive on their estates than with the influx of Irish labourers into burgeoning industrial towns and cities. The bishops of the nineteenth century were less concerned with preserving the low-key approach to their religion of the Catholic gentry than with finding the means of addressing the spiritual, and social, needs of their working-class flocks. In education, as in much else, the broad pattern of the nineteenth-century relationship between the gentry and the Church was one of the gentry staying loyal to Church institutions, but reserving the right to grumble.

There were complaints about the type of education being provided for the sons of the Catholic gentry in the Catholic colleges. Besides the questioning of the quality of teaching and learning on offer, there were objections to the mixing of scions of the gentry with clerical students of lower social standing. A clear example of this view came not from an old Catholic, but a convert, the Oxford-educated lawyer, Edward Bellasis:

> In the existing schools there is too great an admixture
> of classes, many of the scholars coming from homely
> dwellings, bringing with them provincialisms, not to
> say vulgarities, which were perhaps in great measure,
> got rid of by associating with their school fellows, but
> at the cost of leaving a certain portion behind.[38]

Against this background, there were attempts to create schools exclusively for the gentry. The earliest move in this direction came from the Cisalpine Club in 1793. This association of Catholic aristocrats proposed a public school for the sons of Catholic aristocrats and gentlemen, which, while it would have a priest headmaster, would be under lay control. This scheme, however, came to nothing. The Vicars Apostolic would not support it, and the opening of a college at Oscott, where

---

[38] Memorials of Mr Serjeant Bellasis 1800–73, as quoted in McClelland, 'School or Cloister?', p. 121.

clerical and lay students would be taught on the model of the continental colleges, destroyed the prospects of the lay gentry school. The success of Oscott was guaranteed by the securing of Dr Bew, the leading English Catholic academic of the day as its principal; it had been the hope of the Cisalpine Club to acquire Dr Bew.

Thereafter, the Catholic gentry patronized various Catholic institutions established in the later eighteenth and early nineteenth century. The majority, however, tended to use Oscott. As McClelland has commented, 'The nobility were loyal to Oscott and if one looks down the list of students who attended the College from its inception until it ceased to function in 1889, one is particularly struck by the old Catholic names which reappear with constant regularity'.[39] This was especially the case when Nicholas Wiseman was at Oscott. Gentili was rather critical of Wiseman's courting of the Catholic gentry at Oscott, saying that Wiseman, in wanting to make Oscott the Catholic Eton, was too lavish in his treatment of the gentry students. There was a danger that Oscott was 'only a secular college and with little discipline at that'.[40]

Two attempts were made in the second half of the nineteenth century to create Catholic gentry schools. In 1859, Newman tried to establish the Oratory as a school for the Catholic upper classes. In Evennett's view, Newman's

> avowed object was to meet the wishes of many Catholic parents, particularly converts, for a Catholic school on English Public School lines, in touch with the culture of Oxford and Cambridge, which Catholics were not then allowed to attend, and where feminine care and influence, such as were to be seen at that time in the Eton dame system, could be exercised in a manner impossible in ecclesiastical colleges like Oscott or Stonyhurst.[41]

In an ideal world, from Newman's perspective, this would have been a school that, with the approval of the Church, fed

---

[39] *Ibid.*, p. 120.
[40] P. Dennison, 'Thomas Walsh's Vision of Oscott', as quoted in Champ, *Oscott*, p. 76.
[41] Evennett, *The Catholic Schools*, p. 70.

aristocratic Catholics into Oxford. Newman's hopes in this direction came to nothing. The Church remained resolute in the mid-century against allowing Catholics into the ancient Anglican universities and the Oratory School did not become the school of choice for the Catholic gentry. The failure of the Oratory to realize the ambition of its promoters was largely the result of personality clashes. Mrs Wootton, the ex-Eton Dame recruited to the Oratory, could not get on with the headmaster, Fr Darnell, who, as an old boy of Winchester, knew little of the Eton dame system and persisted in treating her as a matron whose only concerns were domestic arrangements. Such disputes, and Newman's general handling of the headmaster and staff, led to Darnell resigning in 1862.[42] The school survived, but after such a difficult beginning, it could not attract sufficient of the old Catholic gentry families away from Oscott and the other schools that they patronized.

A more serious possibility as the Catholic school that would be the school of the gentry was the venture embarked upon by Mgr Petre at Woburn Park. This school was modelled on the Anglican public schools and charged the highest fees of any contemporary Catholic school. It sought to emulate academic standards of the great public schools in the Classics and to give boys the freedoms and responsibilities characteristic of the prefect system. Woburn ran from 1877 until its closure in 1884, managing to secure the endorsement of Cardinal Manning and some academic success: eighteen of its boys went to Oxford. Its failure, however, was less to do with the personality of its founder than chance. The Woburn School was a costly business. Petre was forced to close the school by his father before any more of the family's fortune was dissipated.[43]

In the last quarter of the nineteenth century, therefore, whatever the dissatisfaction which elements of the Catholic gentry might feel about the social and academic shortcomings of

---

[42] For details of the troubles at the Oratory, see Barnes, *Catholic Schools*, pp. 241–2. See also Shrimpton, *Catholic Eton*, pp. 116–24.

[43] McClelland, 'School or Cloister?', p. 127. Woburn's demise is also covered by Shrimpton, *Catholic Eton*, p. 253. The Woburn site was later taken over by the Josephite school, St George's College, Weybridge.

Catholic colleges, they were stuck with institutions such as Oscott. They were denied access to Oxford and Cambridge, and attempts to create Catholic schools modelled on the great Anglican public schools had foundered.

The aristocracy and gentry, however, were to lose the Oscott option as the character of the Catholic colleges concerned with the education of secular priests changed. By the 1890s, and just before the switch in policy to allow Catholics to attend Oxford and Cambridge, lay students were excluded from Oscott and, in effect, forced out of Ushaw. At Ware, the school was separated from the seminary. This was largely the result of the developing policy of the bishops. Bishops wanted diocesan seminaries that were tridentine in plan and organization. They were also of the view that would-be priests should not be educated alongside the laity and thus exposed to worldly influences. In 1857 Bishop Ullathorne had the president of Oscott, Dr Weedall, close the chapel at Oscott to the laity. The laity had a local chapel that they could attend. Newman, who might disagree with Bishop Ullathorne on a range of issues, was also unhappy about the influence of the laity on young clerics during their education. His view of the college at Oscott was that

> A school is a bustling place — divines require something
> more quiet, more strict, more monastic. Oscott is a place
> of dissipation. Tribes of women and hosts of visitors.
> The want of rule is felt even at St Edmund's I suspect,
> but all is disorder at Oscott ... Oscott is a bustling
> thoroughfare.[44]

Regarding episcopal jurisdiction, the English bishops, after the restoration of the hierarchy, had the prospect of moving away from the provisions made during the English Church's missionary period and establishing diocesan seminaries. As Judith Champ has remarked on the discussion of this issue, during the 1855 Second Provincial Synod,

---

[44] Newman to J. D. Dalgairns, 6 July 1846. Cited in P. Dennison, 'Thomas Walsh's Vision of Oscott', as quoted in Champ, *Oscott*, pp. 76–7.

The bishops had two models before them: that of the Council of Trent, which demanded individual seminaries under the sole control of the ordinary and that of the English colleges abroad over which no bishop had sole jurisdiction but to which all contributed support.[45]

Over time, the preference of the bishops for the latter model became clear. Bishop Ullathorne, who, as has been seen in other circumstances, was prepared to defend traditional Catholic educational practice, was happy to countenance change when it came to episcopal jurisdiction over the education of priests. According to Champ, 'Ullathorne often expressed the belief that missionary arrangements which had evolved during the recusant period should be regarded as temporary expedients to be replaced as quickly as possible by the regular forms of ecclesiastical life common to Catholic Europe'.[46] The result of this for Oscott was that in 1873 a diocesan seminary was opened at St Bernard's, Olton. In 1889, however, the new Bishop of Birmingham, Edward Ilsley, decided that Oscott was the better location for the seminary. St Bernard's was closed, its seminarians moved to Oscott and the lay students excluded from Oscott. While Oscott may for some of the Catholic gentry not have been the ideal, the decision still caused considerable anger, as Champ has said: 'It was probably true to say that the heyday of Oscott as a school for the sons of gentlemen was over by 1889 but the laity were furious at the decision to close the college to lay students'.[47]

At Ushaw, things were a little more complicated. In 1876 the College educated a substantial number of lay boys. In that year, there were 168 Church students and 117 lay students. The number of lay students in comparison to Church students fell from this time. In 1884 there were 188 Church students to 59 lay students. In 1884 the decision was taken to charge higher fees for lay students. Thereafter, the number of lay students collapsed. Ushaw became, in effect, exclusively a seminary. The historian of Ushaw, Fr Milburn, has written:

---

[45] Champ, *Oscott*, p. 96.
[46] *Ibid.*, p. 97.
[47] *Ibid.*, p. 103.

From this time forward it may be said that Ushaw made
no further attempt to compete with Catholic schools and
colleges run by Jesuits and Benedictines and other orders
and congregations at Ampleforth, Downside, Stonyhurst
and elsewhere in England ... Inevitably, the reduction
in the number of lay students damaged the prestige
of the college; it became isolated and hidden from the
public gaze. Coming at a time when, educationally, the
college had slipped from the eminence it had attained
during the days of Newsham and Tate, and when the
popularity as well as the standards of the schools run
by religious was increasing quickly, the raising of fees
helped to change in yet another way the character of
the college.[48]

At Ware, Cardinal Manning had removed the theologians from
St Edmund's College to a new seminary at Hammersmith in
1869. St Edmund's remained a school for lay boys only until
1904. Its fortunes in this period were at a low ebb. The lack of
endowments for St Edmund's made it a constant struggle to
keep the school open.[49]

Coming towards the end of the nineteenth century, therefore, there was something of a vacuum developing with regard
to the education of the Catholic gentry. This was a Catholic
gentry, moreover, together with an expanding Catholic middle
class, that was about to be given leave to attend Oxford and
Cambridge and would be looking for suitable schools. This
was the situation that Ampleforth College was to exploit. At
the end of the nineteenth century, however, it was by no means
obvious that Ampleforth would be at the leading edge of those
Catholic schools prepared to abandon the traditional ways of
the Catholic colleges and assimilate those of the Anglican public schools. Ampleforth was a small school operating within
the old Catholic educational tradition.

Ampleforth College managed to survive the defections of
staff and pupils engineered by Bishop Baines, but it lost the
prestige of being a school for the sons of the Catholic aristoc-

[48]   Milburn, *Ushaw*, pp. 289–90.
[49]   Barnes, *Catholic Schools*, pp. 22–4. The seminary returned in 1904 but
remained separate from the school.

racy. The key figure in the school's revival was the prior from 1838 to 1846, Fr Anselm Cockshoot. Cockshoot had attended the school in the days of Fr Augustine Baines and did his best to recover the position enjoyed by the school in those days.[50] Under Prior Cockshoot, initiatives were taken to improve the academic quality of school and community. Towards the end of his time as prior, Fr Anselm Cockshoot was congratulated by the Provincial, Dr Molyneux, on 'the present prosperity' of Ampleforth. As Almond said, Cockshoot 'had the satisfaction to find the school grow in numbers to more than fifty and to see a higher standard of work, discipline and schoolboy comfort, aimed at and attained'.[51]

Under Prior Cockshoot the Ampleforth school did not regain the place within Catholic circles it had enjoyed before 1830, but it was given a sound base for a long-term future. To an extent it became a larger-scale version of the small school that had existed at Dieulouard. Its numbers wavered between fifty and hundred. It drew most of its pupils from the localities served by Ampleforth priests and many of those pupils stayed on to join the monastery (those that did not leave school at fifteen or sixteen to take commercial or professional posts). In the early issues of the *Ampleforth Journal* there is the occasional reference to old boys and their occupations; an example is T. C. Clarke, who became the president of the Midlands Chemists' Assistants' Association in 1896.[52]

In the mid-century the school materially benefited from the enterprise of an energetic and reforming prior, Fr Wilfrid Cooper. Fr Wilfrid had entered Ampleforth as a nine-year-old in 1828. He caught the tail end of the school's period of prosperity and was one of those who stayed with the school through the difficult period as Bishop Baines tried to establish Prior Park. He joined the community in 1835 and as a twenty-year-old deacon in 1839 was made Prefect of the school under Prior Cockshoot. Shortly after his ordination in 1844 he was

---

[50]   Cockshoot appears in several of the exhibition programmes for the 1820s. See above and Ampleforth Abbey Archives, EX01–4, 5, 6.
[51]   Almond, *Ampleforth*, p. 341.
[52]   *Ampleforth Journal*, 2 (1896), p. 352.

sent on the mission to a Liverpool parish. This pattern of the school being the work of young monks until their ordination was typical of the Catholic school tradition. When Fr Wilfrid returned to Ampleforth in 1850 as prior, there were sixteen members of the community in Ampleforth and thirty-one in the parishes.

In his time as prior, Fr Wilfrid embarked upon monastic reform and a programme of building. Taking advantage of the slackening of anti-Catholicism, the monks resumed the wearing of the full Benedictine habit. Exploiting financial windfalls, notably a legacy of £1000 from the Swales family and a donation of £6000 from Br Jerome Whatmore on his profession, Fr Wilfrid was able to engage Joseph Hansom as the architect of a new Abbey Church, built between 1854 and 1857, and a new school building, completed between 1859 and 1861. The total spent on the new school alone was £1300. This level of spending alarmed the Ampleforth community. In 1862, Fr Wilfrid Cooper was criticized for financial imprudence. In 1863, citing health reasons, he stood down as prior. Fr Wilfrid spent the rest of his life, until 1877, working in the parishes, mostly in the docklands of Liverpool.[53]

Notwithstanding the work of Fr Wilfrid Cooper, the school that he left at Ampleforth was not of sufficient importance to attract the attention of the Taunton Commission's enquiries. The Jesuit schools of Stonyhurst and Mount St Mary's were the subject of reports, as was St Mary's, Oscott. The Benedictine schools of Ampleforth and Downside were ignored.[54] The absence of Ampleforth from the Taunton Commission is a pity for there are few school records in the Abbey archives, apart from some correspondence about Fr Wilfrid's building pro- gramme, for the second half of the nineteenth century. Ample- forth, like other schools, has a patchy collection of records.[55]

---

[53] See Fr Bernard Green, 'Wilfrid Cooper OSB, Prior 1850–1863', *Ampleforth Journal*, 94 (1989), pp. 4–11.

[54] Taunton Commission. Parliamentary Papers, 1867–8, XXVIII, Part xv, Yorkshire and Northern Counties. Ampleforth is not mentioned, but Stonyhurst (part xiv), Mount St Mary's (xiii) and Oscott (vii) are.

[55] For an example of the absence of records causing difficulties for historians, see Rubenstein looking for empirical evidence to test the

Something of the life of the school in this period, however, can be seen in the *Ampleforth Journal*, started in 1895. The Journal gives an understanding of the overall character of the school through occasional reporting of school activity, articles which hark back to earlier days, and the obituaries of members of the community. A school journal cannot be expected to reveal the negative aspects of school life; the extent of bullying, the degree of tedium experienced in class or the frequency, and perhaps injustice, of punishments. Notwithstanding the limitations of the *Ampleforth Journal* as a source, however, it gives a plausible picture of Ampleforth approaching the end of the century, within its traditional points of reference, harmonious and successful. In the Journal there are records of theatrical rehearsals, including musicals, debates, sporting fixtures and successes in school certificate examinations. There was no Officer Training Corps[56] but there was drilling as a means of disciplined exercise. A Sgt Major Greaves had started this when recruited by the school in 1867.[57] In the school's games, young monk teachers frequently took the field with the boys. In 1896, for example, an Ampleforth association football team, accompanied by some twenty boys and masters as supporters, watched four of the brethren play in a 5–1 win over Malton Swifts.[58] This success may have been due in some part to exploitation of Ampleforth's Liverpool connections. The previous year, 'Mr J. Ross and Mr Becton, well known professionals of the Liverpool eleven and both late of Preston North End came for a few days to coach our football team.

argument of Martin Wiener set out in *English Culture and the Decline of the Industrial Spirit*, that public schools were hostile to the business community in England, Rubenstein found that Eton kept no alumni records after 1910 and 'no school in the North of England likely to attract significant numbers of businessmen's sons possessed a usable alumni directory'. W. D. Rubenstein, *Capitalism, Culture and Decline in Britain, 1750–1990* (London: Routledge, 1993), p. 106.

56 The OTC was established at Ampleforth in 1911. See Ampleforth Abbey Archives, NX57 7M12, Fr Columba Cary-Elwes, Nevill Biography, version 3, p. 43.
57 *Ampleforth Journal*, 2 (1896), p. 36.
58 *Ibid.*, p. 344.

They thoroughly reorganized the methods of attack and this proved a very great advantage.'[59]

An interesting and illustrative monastic obituary is that of Fr Austin Bury from 1904.[60] Fr Austin Bury, Abbot Bury by the time of his death (he was made titular abbot of Evesham in 1888) was an important figure in the history of the school and community. Teaching in the school, briefly, after his profession in 1844, and then from 1848 to 1860, Fr Austin Bury helped form the next generation of Ampleforth monks; those who were to be the key figures in the debates about the future of education for the Catholic community and the part to be played by Ampleforth. Notable amongst his pupils was Bishop Hedley, the Ampleforth monk who did much to secure the permission for Catholics to attend Oxford and Cambridge and who encouraged the early moves at Ampleforth to turn the school into an effective feeder to these universities.

Fr Austin Bury was educated in the post-Baines Ampleforth and professed a monk in 1844. Shortly after his profession, as an eighteen-year-old, Fr Austin had taught in the school. His obituarist, Fr Wilfrid Brown, recalled being taught Corneille and Racine by Fr Austin in his Poetry year. This in itself is of interest, showing that the breadth of the Ampleforth curriculum reflected the school under Fr Augustine Baines. Poetry at Ampleforth saw the boys studying more than the work of classical authors. Prior Cockshoot, however, sought to improve the academic quality of the school and community by sending two of his brightest young men to acquire a university education. Brs Austin Bury and Laurence Shepherd were sent to Parma, where they studied from 1845 to 1848. On their return, they taught the senior boys in the school.

Fr Austin effected some change in the school's programme of studies. Bishop Hedley recalled that Fr Austin

> brought back with him a thorough knowledge and enthusiastic appreciation of the philosophy of St Thomas Aquinas and the strict Thomistic school represented by Cardinal Cajetan and Joannes a Santo. Before this

59   *Ibid.*, p. 218.
60   *Ampleforth Journal*, 10 (1904), p. 238.

66

time metaphysical philosophy at Ampleforth had been represented by such writers as Locke, Watts, Reid and Stewart—as at other Colleges in England.[61]

Fr Austin also returned with a manuscript of the work of one of his teachers, the Jesuit theologian Sordi. Copies of this were made by the senior Ampleforth students for subsequent teaching. When innovation was made in the Ampleforth studies, it drew on continental Catholic scholarship.

Bishop Hedley was at the top of the school in 1853–4 and was taught by Fr Austin. It is interesting that only five students were in what was, in effect, the Sixth Form. Only one of Bishop Hedley's fellow students was a layman, Thomas Byron. The others became Fr Oswald Tyndall, Fr Benedict Murphy and Fr Ildefonsus Brown. From the 1850s until the last quarter of the nineteenth century, about half the boys in the school were intended for the monastery. In 1874, forty-two of the eighty boys in the school were church students.[62]

It was during this time of Fr Austin Bury's teaching that the magazine, *The Student*, appeared in 1853. This publication dealt with issues such as 'Style', 'The Sublime' and 'Scepticism'. In the course of the articles, there was critical discussion of Burke, Kant and Macaulay. In the judgment of Fr Cuthbert Almond, writing in 1903 and comparing *The Student* with the Ampleforth student journalism of his own day,

> the writers of *The Student* attacked their subjects as if they were really familiar with them ... the essays are adequate enough to prove that the students of those days gave time and thought to abstract studies and did not merely take them up to make copy out of them.[63]

No matter how good a scholar and inspiring teacher Fr Austin was, however, he was not kept in the school. In 1860 he was

---

[61] *Ibid.*, p. 238
[62] See J. McCann, 'The Nineteenth Century', in McCann and Cary-Elwes, *Ampleforth and its Origins*, p. 226. General Chapter Reports, in the keeping of the abbot of Ampleforth, give the number of church students from 1854.
[63] Almond, *Ampleforth*, p. 358, and Ampleforth Abbey Archives, DX 09 6 7J13, *The Student*, 1853.

sent on the mission. Building schools and churches in the Lancashire parishes, as Fr Austin did in Hindley and Warrington, was still the principal work of Ampleforth.[64]

---

[64] *Ampleforth Journal*, 10 (1904), p. 238.

5

Ampleforth
in the Twentieth Century

I T HAS ALREADY BEEN SEEN THAT, amongst the religious communities that ran the Catholic schools in the nineteenth century, there was a growing sense of dissatisfaction with what was being provided academically in their schools. Catholic schools may have had broader curricula than the Anglican public schools, but providing boys with expertise in arithmetic was not seen as having the kudos of the classical scholarship on offer at Eton and Winchester. When the Catholic communities took advantage of the lifting of the Church's ban on Oxford and Cambridge, this sense of the inferiority of Catholic academic life became intensified as the first young monks and priests studied in the ancient universities. The sense that Oxford provided the highest level of academic study, and that their own schooling had not prepared them properly for this, certainly in comparison with young men coming from Winchester, can be seen in the reactions of the young Ampleforth monks sent to Hunter Blair's Hall in Oxford. These graduates returned from Oxford keen to raise the standing of their schools.

From the perspective of Catholic parents, new educational choices became available following the opening of Oxford and Cambridge. The Catholic aristocracy and gentry could now complete the academic (and social) education of their sons in the same institutions as their Anglican peers. It was unlikely that this opportunity would be neglected. Moreover, the upwardly mobile Catholic middle class could now aspire to an Oxford or Cambridge education for its sons. There would now be a demand for secondary schools up to the task of preparing Catholic youths for the ancient universities.

In some respects, the obvious schools for this purpose were the existing Anglican schools. The leading Anglican public schools were feeders of the Oxbridge colleges. As has been recently pointed out by Peter Snow, 'Oxford in the 1890s was much smaller (about a quarter of today's 11,000 undergraduates) and of course highly exclusive. The Clarendon (top nine) public schools supplied almost a third of its intake.'[1] While there is some anecdotal evidence of anti-Catholicism at Winchester,[2] other Clarendon schools were willing to take Catholic students of the right social background, as were Oxford and Cambridge colleges. The whole tenor of opinion towards Catholicism in the world of which the Anglican public schools were a part began to soften in late Victorian England. As Norman has argued, 'Towards the end of the nineteenth century educated opinion began to demonstrate an increasing tolerance towards Roman Catholicism ... Roman Catholics were in reality getting an increasing amount of tolerant consideration from ... society'.[3] If, in this climate, the leading Anglican schools were prepared to admit Catholic boys, the need to deprive Catholic parents of the excuse for sending their sons to such schools became an important issue for those seeking to preserve the existing Catholic schools. It gave added urgency to those wishing to assimilate the ways and standards of what were perceived as the best schools in the country. This motive for the emulation of the Anglican schools was clearly stated by Fr Paul Nevill:

> Abbot Edmund [Matthews] had clear views and a definite policy which he required those whom he put in

[1]   P. Snow, 'Decadent Decade?', *Oxford Today*, 12/1 (1999), p. 11.
[2]   Hugh Codrington, sometime Director of Admissions and later housemaster at Ampleforth College, tells the story of his grandfather being expelled from Winchester before the Great War because he had converted to Catholicism. Hugh's father was sent to Ampleforth, where he became head monitor under Fr Paul Nevill. There is no documentary evidence at Winchester to confirm this.
[3]   E. R. Norman, *Anti-Catholicism in Victorian England* (London: Allen and Unwin, 1968), p. 20.

charge of the school to carry through. We were to give
the Catholics of this country a school comparable in
training, scholastic achievements and numbers with the
best in the country, so that there could be no excuse for
sending their sons to a non-Catholic school. The training
was to be on traditional English lines, so long as nothing
clashed with that strong and manly Catholicism which
we owed to our own early connexion with Lancashire.[4]

As headmaster in 1920, Fr Edmund had made this point at the
important Extraordinary Conventual Chapter of the Ampleforth community, which approved in principle many of the
changes necessary to allow the development of the school on
public school lines. At the conclusion of a justification of the
monitorial and house systems Fr Edmund said that

It would prove a great attraction to very many parents
more especially to converts many of whom were
wedded to the system from the remembrance of their
experiences in the large public schools. It would certainly
be removing one of the incentives to sending their boys
to Protestant schools.[5]

Fr Edmund was right about the attractiveness of such a change
to Catholic parents. Once Catholic schools such as Ampleforth
started to adopt the ways of the established public schools,
it did not take for large numbers of wealthy Catholics to
turn away from Anglican schools for their sons' pre-univer-
sity education. While Catholics were increasingly tolerated
from the second half of the nineteenth century and became
more involved in the wider society of Britain, they also firmly
retained a separate identity. Historians of the Catholic community in later Victorian and Edwardian Britain have remarked
upon this, largely in the context of the predominantly Irish

---

[4]   P. Nevill, 'Modern Ampleforth', in McCann and Cary-Elwes,
      Ampleforth and its Origins, p. 257.
[5]   Archives of the Abbot of Ampleforth Abbey, Minutes of the
      Extraordinary Conventual Chapter, 13–14 April 1920. Minutes of
      Chapter meetings are kept by the abbot of Ampleforth and are not in
      the archives of the monastic library. I am grateful to the then Fr Abbot,
      Fr Timothy Wright, for access to the minutes of the 1920 meeting.

Catholic working-class world of the industrial towns. Catholics can be found participating in trade-union and political activity with non-Catholics but keeping a strong sense of their own identity and institutions. While Nonconformist elementary school building, for example, declined as increasing use was made of state school provision, the Catholic Church made strenuous efforts to keep, and increase, its own schools.[6] McLeod has referred to the creation and maintenance of a ghetto mentality amongst late Victorian Catholics.[7] Parsons summed this up:

> Such exclusiveness had its ironic aspects: as the Victorian period saw a steady increase in the basic acceptance of the Roman Catholic presence in Britain, the Roman Catholic response was to construct a community with hard edges and a markedly separate identity. But that irony was in turn part of a larger paradox.[8]

Victorian Catholicism, as Norman has observed, was remarkably astute in its seizure of the opportunity offered by the emergence of a liberal pluralist state, but it exploited the opportunity by virtue of its disciplined non-liberalism and non-pluralism. While aristocratic, gentry and upper middle-class Catholicism was a small and, in many respects, atypical part of the Catholic Church, it is possible to fit it into this context. Wealthy Catholics might want access to Oxford and Cambridge; they might want access to and acceptance in the professions, the armed services and the higher reaches of society; but they also wanted to maintain their Catholic identity. Schools such as Ampleforth adapting sufficiently to a changing world made this possible. In this context, it is interesting to note the appearance of Fr A.

---

6   G. Parsons, *Religion in Victorian Britain, Vol. I, Traditions* (Manchester: Manchester University Press, 1988), p. 180.
7   H. McLeod, 'Building the Catholic Ghetto', in W. J. Sheils and D. Wood (eds), *Voluntary Religion* (Oxford: Oxford University Press, 1986).
8   Parsons, *Religion*, p.180. See also, E. R. Norman, *The English Roman Catholic Church in the Nineteenth Century* (Oxford: Oxford University Press, 1984) and E. R. Norman, *Roman Catholicism in England from the Elizabethan Settlement to the Second Vatican Council* (Oxford: Oxford University Press, 1985).

S. Barnes's book *The Catholic Schools of England* in 1926.[9] This publication came just at the time when Fr Paul Nevill, in the early days of his headmastership, was pushing through the changes that would see Ampleforth resemble an English public school in much of its structures and ethos. Barnes's book emphasized the long history of English Catholic education and the continuities of the mediaeval educational tradition in the modern world. It argued that the tradition of mediaeval (and Catholic) Winchester and Eton had been carried on by the English Catholic schools on the continent and had been brought back to England, and further developed, by the Benedictines and Jesuits at Ampleforth, Downside and Stonyhurst. Just how many Catholic parents about to decide on the school for their son would have read Barnes's book is a moot point, but it does seem fair to see his book as contributing to a climate in which Catholic public schools were likely to be supported by their own community, whatever the attractions of the famous Anglican schools. As the reviewer of Barnes's work in the *Times Literary Supplement* commented, 'His book will be of unique value to the Catholic parent who, notwithstanding his Bishops, wavers between sending his boys to a Roman or Anglican public school'.[10]

Before looking in detail at the successful transformation of Ampleforth from a small, and somewhat obscure, northern school into a leading English public school, it is worth considering other Catholic independent schools at the start of the twentieth century from the perspectives of their relative standing within the world of Catholic education and their prospects for being accepted into, and moving up, the ranks of the public schools.

Stonyhurst was the largest, best-known and most accepted as a public school of the Catholic institutions. In Honey's analysis of the public schools in 1902, there were fifty schools in what he called Class A. No Catholic school was included in this category, although Stonyhurst was in Class B with

9 Barnes, *Catholic Schools.*
10 *Times Literary Supplement,* 4 December 1926.

another Jesuit school, Beaumont, not far behind.[11] By 1939 there had been a dramatic change. The public school world had seen considerable expansion. In Honey's view, of the new schools,

> By far the biggest category of schools were the Nonconformist and Roman Catholic schools, so sparsely represented in classes A or B by 1902, yet by 1939 constituting among the most expensive of the schools in the HMC and completely accepted as public schools by all other public school criteria, including games interaction. The massive non-Anglican breakthrough into the public school community was presaged by the first appearance at the very end of the nineteenth century by Downside and six other Roman Catholic schools competing for the first time in the largely public school world of the Oxford and Cambridge Higher Certificate examination. The change in the character and status of such schools as these between the Victorian period and our own are a significant commentary on the sociology of Roman Catholicism and Protestant Nonconformists in the last hundred years.[12]

The striking advances made by Downside and Ampleforth in this period, and the relative loss of place by Stonyhurst, can be seen in the size of the schools. According to Bamford, Ampleforth was the fastest-growing public school between 1919 and 1936.[13] The relative standing of the three leading Catholic schools, by numbers of pupils, from the mid-nineteenth to the mid-twentieth centuries, can be seen in the following table, taken from Bamford's work on the rank order by pupil numbers of the ninety-four schools counted by him as public schools.

---

[11]   Honey, *Tom Brown's Universe*, p. 285.
[12]   *Ibid.*, p. 287.
[13]   Bamford, *The Rise of the Public Schools*, pp. 27–8.

Ampleforth, Stonyhurst and Downside in Rank Order
by Pupil Numbers in the Public Schools.[14]

	1866	1881	1900	1919	1936	1962
Ampleforth	48	55	53	37	14	12
Stonyhurst	11	16	16	15	24	37
Downside	35	39	39	33	37	15

Regarding the absolute sizes of the schools, the position, according to Bamford, was as below:

Size of School 1919–62:
Ampleforth, Stonyhurst and Downside.[15]

	1919	1936	1962
Ampleforth	170	450	550
Stonyhurst	330	300	350
Downside	190	225	520

Numbers alone do not reveal the whole picture, but they do give an indication of which schools are standing still, which are declining and which are progressing. The numbers, of course, say nothing about the status accorded to the schools. The impression here, however, is that the Benedictines of Ampleforth and Downside were capturing the Catholic aristocracy and, in the wake of this, raising their schools' social standing as well as increasing their numbers. Schools that largely conformed to the ethos of the Anglican schools and which contained the family members of the Duke of Norfolk, the Marquess of Bute, and the like, were going to be accepted amongst the elite of the public school world. The extent to which Catholics could be integrated into the aristocratic world, and the success of Ampleforth within this, is illustrated in P. J. Rich's study of the role played by the public schools in the expansion and maintenance of the British Empire. He observes:

Ampleforth is always well represented in English
royal and state ceremonial with the present Duke of

---

[14]   *Ibid.*, p.11.
[15]   *Ibid.*

Norfolk as Earl Marshal of England, Sir John Johnston as Comptroller of the Lord Chamberlain's Office, Maj. General Lord Fitzalan Howard as Gold Stick to the Queen, Henry Paston Bedingfield as Rouge Croix Pursuivant at the College of Arms.[16]

In gaining the support of the Catholic gentry, however, Stonyhurst was at something of a disadvantage. Part of Stonyhurst's difficulty in this respect was the element of distrust towards the Jesuits that had long been apparent in some old Catholic gentry circles. The Jesuits did not have a good record when it came to being amenable to the influence of the English Catholic gentry. It was feared that, in their schools, the Jesuits were mainly concerned with the recruitment of the next generation of the Society. Moreover, the degree of supervision and severity of punishment in Jesuit schools was deemed excessive.[17] There was an irony in the nineteenth century of the Jesuits at Stonyhurst being at the forefront of trying to compete academically with the Anglican public schools in the Classics, in the hope, in least in part, that this would bring the Catholic gentry back to the support of the College, while the long-term beneficiaries of this were the Benedictines.

Stonyhurst was not helped either by the Jesuits being the least willing of the Catholic orders to abandon Catholic educational tradition in the pursuit of acceptance within the public school world. Stonyhurst became more focused on the winning of Oxbridge scholarships; more monitorial power was given to its boys; and the cult of games with its trappings of house colours and the rest developed considerably. However, it did not abandon the Playroom system, the organization of its forms by the old names of Syntax, Poetry and Rhetoric. Stonyhurst, in spite of moving towards the Anglican public schools, still appeared much more of a Catholic college run on traditional lines than its Benedictine rivals at Ampleforth and Downside. Moreover, the Jesuit refusal to move from the

---

[16] P. J. Rich, *Elixir of Empire* (London: Regency Press, 1989), p. 72.
[17] For discussion of the difficulties the Jesuits encountered with the English aristocracy see McClelland, 'School or Cloister?', and McClelland, *English Roman Catholics*, pp. 38–9, 120.

Playroom system limited the ability of Stonyhurst to expand and take advantage of the increasing demand from Catholic families in the twentieth century for a public school education. A horizontal year group becomes difficult to supervise once there are more than fifty or sixty boys: the house system allows for much more flexibility. Once the Benedictine schools adopted the house system, all they had to do to expand was to open new houses. The Jesuit approach to expansion in the nineteenth century had been to open new schools. The Jesuits had opened day schools for the urban Catholic middle class such as Wimbledon College and St Michael's, Leeds. They had also opened boarding schools: Mount St Mary's and Beaumont.

Beaumont had the potential to become a leading public school and to an extent realized this. Beaumont was originally a Jesuit Seminary but in 1861 was run as a school when the novices moved to Roehampton. By the turn of the century, it attracted a sprinkling of peers' sons and some scions of the Spanish aristocracy.[18] Unlike Stonyhurst it did not use traditional Catholic terms for its year groups; it had fewer distinctive Catholic traditions to defend than Stonyhurst. By the 1940s it had acquired something of a reputation for games (its Windsor location gave it the chance to row and play soccer against Eton)[19] and the acquisition of Oxford and Cambridge scholarships. Evennett, when writing to Fr Paul Nevill about the Catholic public schools in 1943, implied that Stonyhurst, Ampleforth, Downside and Beaumont were the leading Catholic public schools. Fr Paul bridled at this, especially the suggestion that Beaumont was on a par with Ampleforth.[20] Whatever its pretensions and successes, Beaumont did not have the prestige of origins in continental exile, and its Jesuit commitment to the playroom system meant that it would never be a large school.

---

[18] Honey, *Tom Brown's Universe*, p. 293. See also P. Levi, *Beaumont* (London: Andre Deutsch, 1961).

[19] Barnes, *Catholic Schools*, p. 181.

[20] Ampleforth Abbey Archives, DX 65, Letter from H. O. Evennett to Fr P. Nevill, 15 September 1943. Reply from Fr P. Nevill, 24 September 1943.

Jesuit involvement in the public school world did not quite have the potential of the Benedictines. The Jesuits ran a range of schools and Jesuit teachers were at the service of an order operating worldwide and with concerns beyond those of education. The Benedictines operated in stable communities and, while their responsibilities also extended to parish work, when it came to public schools, they were only concerned with one school. An abbot and headmaster, with the backing of their community, could, as was the case eventually at Ampleforth, effect radical change in the direction of their school. In this context, two Benedictine communities, Belmont and Douai, provide an interesting constraint to the development of the school at Ampleforth.

At Belmont there was never any intention to become a major public school. The monastery at Belmont opened in 1859 and from 1860 until 1874 ran a small preparatory school that rarely had more than twenty boys. The decision to open a school was taken in 1924, in no small part to help the monastic community financially.[21] The school opened in 1926 with eleven pupils under the headmastership of Dom Anselm Lightbond. In the 1930s the school peaked at 50 boys and in the 1940s the school achieved numbers in the nineties. It was not until the 1960s, however, that the school moved into the hundreds. This period of expansion was under the headmastership of Dom Roger Hosker, appointed in 1961. He reorganized the school by revising its rules, tightening discipline, streaming classes and emphasizing sports. He aimed at a school of 250 students. The school did increase in numbers and Fr Hosker was able to fund the building of a new boarding house to add to the three houses in existing buildings.[22] Even in this phase of expansion, however, there was no aspiration that Belmont should rise in the ranks of the English public schools. The school never sought membership of the HMC.

Things were a little different at Douai. The monastic house established at Woolhampton, Berkshire, in 1903 had a history

---

[21]   A. Berry OSB (ed.), *Belmont Abbey, Celebrating 150 Years* (Leominster: Gracewing, 2012), p. 209.
[22]   *Ibid.*, p. 214.

to match that of the communities at Ampleforth and Downside. The monks at Woolhampton could trace their community's history back to St Edmund's, the English house established
in Paris in 1615. Expelled from France at the time of The Revolution, and settling at Ware, some members of the community had returned to France, when circumstances allowed in
1818, and re-established an English community in Douai until
expelled again under anti-clerical laws passed in the early
twentieth century. Invited to the diocese of Portsmouth by
Bishop Cahill, the Douai monks settled at Woolhampton. The
new Douai also established a school by merging the existing
Portsmouth Junior Seminary, established in 1882 at St Mary's,
Woolhampton with the remnants of their school at Douai, St
Edmund's. St Mary's itself was based on a small Catholic school
set up in the 1830s.

A school run by the Douai community would have the
potential to match those at Ampleforth and Downside. This
had occurred to some of the Douai community monks, but this
was not the path taken. In his history of Douai School, Abbot
Geoffrey Scott notes:

> The grandiose schemes of a small minority in 1903
> to develop quickly another great public school were
> frankly unrealistic; buildings were inadequate, academic
> standards in terms of classical education, lowish, the
> community was small, young and untrained and there
> was little money.[23]

The school at Douai did, however, become a public school. It
was admitted to the HMC in 1920. Its numbers, however, were
deliberately kept low, to ensure that the school would operate
within the Catholic educational tradition and to maintain the
closeness of school and monastery. Douai's headmaster from
1915 to 1952 was Fr Ignatius Rice. In the view of Fr Geoffrey
Scott, 'He was determined to preserve the familiarity that had
existed between the monks and the boys at the old Douai, at the
cost of lessening the impact a larger school might have made

---

[23] *Douai 1903 to Woolhampton 2003, A Centenary History*, p. 33. Available
online at: http://www.douaiabbey.org.uk/centenary-history.html.

on the national and Catholic educational scene'. Fr Ignatius had stated that he had 'no ambition nor intention to build up an enormous school which might become, like so many others, a big business concern'.[24] By the time of his retirement as headmaster, the school had 150 boys, had not adopted the house system and still followed the modified Jesuit system of the old Douai. In the 1930s, Fr Ignatius was congratulated by David Matthew, later a bishop and Apostolic Delegate for Africa, that, in his view, 'no Catholic school has been so free from the influence of Arnold of Rugby as Douai has been'.[25]

Douai did become more like an English public school when led by Fr Ignatius's successor, Fr Alphonsus Tierney, head-master from 1952 to 1973. Under him, the house system was adopted, more lay staff appointed and a determined effort was made to improve the school's academic status through achieving success in public examinations.[26] Numbers increased but Douai remained a small school of no more than 250. As a minor public school, Douai enjoyed success on its own terms, but in the 1990s it succumbed to the pressures exerted against small rural boarding schools. At Ampleforth, however, in the decade after the establishment of Douai at Woolhampton, decisions were taken that would see its transformation from a rather small school operating within the established Catholic educational tradition into a major school capable of rising into the upper echelon of the English public school hierarchy. The three most important figures in this were Fr Anselm Burge, Fr Edmund Matthews (later Abbot Matthews) and Fr Paul Nevill.

The breakthrough of Ampleforth as a leading public school is usually associated with its headmaster from 1924 until his death in 1954, Fr Paul Nevill, as can be seen in the comment of his history tutor at Oxford, Sir Ernest Barker, in his contribution to the obituaries written for Fr Paul in 1954. Barker wrote, 'Ampleforth College prospered under him: it became one of the

---

24   *Ibid.*, p. 40
25   Douai Society, *School History*. Available online at: http://douaisociety. org/History.htm.
26   Abbot Geoffrey Scott, *Centenary History of Douai Abbey* (Woolhampton: Douai Abbey, 2003), p. 40.

foremost schools in successes won at Oxford, while at the same time its Rugby team became the Dulwich of the North'.[27] In extreme form, the attribution of Ampleforth's success to Fr Paul Nevill can be seen in the assertion of Bence-Jones that 'Father Paul was perhaps the greatest headmaster of his time ... Under his headmastership, Ampleforth became pre-eminent among English Catholic public schools; taking the place formerly occupied by Downside and before that by Stonyhurst.'[28]

Fr Paul's achievement, however, was built on foundations laid by his predecessor, Fr Edmund Matthews, headmaster from 1903 to 1924. The relationship between the two, and the debt owed by Fr Paul to Fr Edmund, was acknowledged by the biographer of Fr Paul, Fr Columba Cary-Elwes:[29]

> This is the life of Fr Paul and there is the almost inevitable danger of it appearing that he was the prime mover in the creation of Ampleforth in its fundamentals as we know it. That would be false. He was the continuer of the work begun by Fr Edmund Matthews. They shared a common ideal. The latter was for going slowly, Fr Paul for forging ahead. Fr Edmund went cautiously because of lack of money and also because he had first to win to his side those older Fathers, mostly on the parishes, but who had a say at Chapter in the destinies of Ampleforth in all its aspects ... It was undoubtedly

[27]   *The Times*, 27 February 1954.
[28]   M. Bence-Jones, *The Catholic Families* (London: Constable, 1995), p. 307.
[29]   Shortly after Fr Paul's death, Fr Columba was commissioned by the abbot to write a life of Fr Paul. Three versions were drafted but none published. In a note left in the Abbey Archives, dated 4 April 1961, Fr Columba said that marks 1 and 2 of his biography were in St Louis Priory, USA. Mark 3 was in Ampleforth. Two draft versions of the biography and associated materials, survive in the Ampleforth Abbey Archives, one in BX05–8, the other in NX5/ /M12. It would seem that one of the St Louis copies found its way back to England. I have referred to these as version 1 and version 2 respectively. Another biography was commissioned from Robert Speaight in the early 1960s. This too did not come to fruition but some of the relevant materials are also kept in the Ampleforth Abbey Archives. The Speaight material is in BX5–03 7M12.

Fr Edmund who pulled Ampleforth out of the slough
... The pioneer and architect of victory.[30]

Both Fr Edmund Matthews and Fr Paul Nevill, in their turn,
owed much to Fr Anselm Burge, prior 1885–99. Both had been
early beneficiaries of the decision to allow Catholics to attend
Oxford and were sent by Prior Burge to take degrees at Hunter
Blair's Hall, later St Benet's Hall. Fr Edmund Matthews read
Classics, and Fr Paul later followed, reading history. Fr Paul
drew attention to the important part played by Prior Burge
in the course of correspondence with Evennett. Towards the
end of the Second World War, Evennett was working for the
Intelligence Services at Bletchley on leave of absence from Trinity College, Cambridge, and preparing a history of Catholic
education to be published in 1944.[31] Replying to a query from
Evennett about the expansion of Ampleforth, Fr Paul wrote:

> The man who ought not to be left out of any account of
> Ampleforth's development is Prior Burge. He was the
> real instigator here of school reform and his ideas had
> their inspiration from Lord Petre and his experiment at
> Woburn Park. Moreover, he founded the Oxford House,
> St Benet's Hall and it was he who sent Abbot Matthews
> there to start it.[32]

As a young monk Fr Anselm had been one of two Benedictines
loaned out to Mgr Petre's school at Woburn. The other was a
Downside monk, Fr Bede Cox. Fr Anselm had also been secretary to Bishop Hedley.[33] Fr Anselm, therefore, had seen how
a Catholic school modelled on the Anglican public schools
and designed to cater for the gentry might work, and had
been a close associate of one of the bishops, the Amplefordian
Bishop Hedley, who was keen to push for Catholic gentry to
attend the ancient universities. It is no surprise that, as prior,

[30]   Ampleforth Abbey Archives, BX05–8, Fr Columba Cary-Elwes,
      untitled biography of Fr Paul Nevill, version 1, p. 67.
[31]   Evennett, *The Catholic Schools*.
[32]   Ampleforth Abbey Archives, DX65. This is a box containing several
      packets of the correspondence of Fr Paul Nevill. Letter from Fr P.
      Nevill to H. O. Evennett, 24 September 1943.
[33]   McCann and Cary-Elwes, *Ampleforth*, p. 239.

Fr Anselm Burge was behind initiatives designed to improve the academic qualifications of his brethren and began to put Ampleforth into a position where it could feed Oxford and Cambridge. Prior Burge was also active in the establish of a Conference of Catholic Colleges that sought a co-ordinated response to the Bryce Commission's Report on Secondary Education, and, with the exception of Ushaw, continued the Catholic move away from association with the qualifications of the University of London and towards those of Oxford and Cambridge. There was also agreement with the proposition of Scott Coward, the Senior Inspector of Training Colleges, that more teachers in Catholic schools should take degrees from Oxford and Cambridge.[34] Fr Anselm Burge, however, was not able to see through his initiatives. Change in the direction of the school was not fully supported by the Ampleforth community. In 1899 Fr Anselm was succeeded in election by Fr Oswald Smith and it was Fr Oswald who was to become the first abbot of Ampleforth when Ampleforth and Downside were both raised to the status of independent abbeys in 1900.

Before looking in detail at how Fr Edmund Matthews and Fr Paul Nevill set about transforming the school, it is important to examine the resistance to altering the school that existed within the monastic community. Studying the opposition to the changes that were to see Ampleforth become a leading English public school is not easy. There clearly were a considerable number of dissidents within the Ampleforth community when it came to changing the ethos, structure and size of the school. One of the features of Ampleforth's development was the slow pace at which change was effected. Burge started things moving in the 1890s but his efforts were temporarily halted under Abbot Oswald Smith. There was school reform and growth under Fr Edmund Matthews from 1903, as will be seen, but these reforms were limited and the slow pace of change was intensely frustrating for the more radical younger brethren. Fr Columba recorded that a group comprising Fr

---

[34] An account of the first meeting of the Conference of Catholic Colleges is given in the *Ampleforth Journal*, 2 (July 1896). The discussion of educational qualifications is on p. 41.

Placid Dolan, Fr Ambrose Byrne, Fr Bernard McElligott and Fr Stephen Marwood, would meet in the old school building, in what became the St Bede's House Gallery, to discuss 'the lifting up of Ampleforth from its complacent rut . . . its Northern roughness, its philistinism'.[35] Especially frustrated was Fr Paul Nevill. In 1910 he had a breakdown and had to be relieved of all teaching. Fr Columba believed this principally the result of anxiety induced by family matters, but not unconnected to the slowness of innovation in the school. In Fr Columba's words, 'He was over eager perhaps for reform'.[36] From 1912 Fr Paul was well enough to be sub-prior and to edit the *Ampleforth Journal*. From 1914 he was parish priest in Ampleforth village and did some teaching in the school, but until 1924 he was, according to Fr Columba, 'outside the swim of things'.[37] Fr Paul in these years worked out the theories concerning how Ampleforth should be changed and how it might be made the leading Catholic public school. Even when the decision in principle was accepted by the community to adopt the house system in 1920, and to expand the school, changes in practice did not come until 1924. It was not until Fr Edmund Matthews was elected as abbot in 1924 and appointed Fr Paul Nevill as headmaster that the pace of change quickened and Ampleforth ascended the ranks of the public-school world.

Detailed information as to why the brakes were so often applied in Ampleforth's transition from a small school run on traditional Catholic lines to a leading English public school is difficult to come by. It is something of a cliché that history is the propaganda of the victors, but in the case of Ampleforth this is largely true. Most of the evidence relating to the school in the crucial first half of the twentieth century comes from those who actively advocated change and were instrumental in bringing

[35]   Ampleforth Abbey Archives, BX05–8, Fr Cary-Elwes, untitled biography of Fr Paul Nevill, version 1, p. 64. The old school building was the original centre of the school based on the house given over to the surviving Dieulouard community in 1802 by Fr Anselm Bolton. It was replaced by a new central building in 1988. Gallery is the Ampleforth term for a floor in a House or classroom area.

[36]   *Ibid.*, p. 53

[37]   *Ibid.*, p. 54.

it about, or those who were products of the changed school. The history of the school published in 1952 was edited by Frs Justin McCann and Columba Cary-Elwes. Both supported the Ampleforth developed by Fr Paul. The chapter on 'Modern Ampleforth' was written by Fr Paul himself. There is also the unpublished biography of Fr Paul by Fr Columba. Much of the archive material relating to the school and Fr Paul was put together by Fr Columba. Key articles in the *Ampleforth Journal*, edited before the Great War by Fr Paul, came from proponents of expansion and change at Ampleforth, as can be seen in the 1912 contributions of Bishop Hedley, Fr Edmund Matthews and Fr Paul.[38] Fr Paul was also responsible for writing the minutes of Council and Chapter meetings.

The opponents of change do not get to speak for themselves in the records, but something can be discerned about the opposition to change from the comments of the ultimately successful reformers. Some opposition was due to fear of financial risk. Writing of the Extraordinary Conventual Chapter of 1920, when the decision to expand the school and adopt the house system was taken, Fr Columba wrote of 'an unexpected ally' emerging in the person of Fr Bede Turner. Fr Bede had been appointed procurator in 1902 and held this post until 1934.[39] Fr Bede 'came forward on the financial side as a champion of expansion'. It seems reasonable to infer from this that finance had been a subject of contention. Coming from the community's Lancashire heartland and previously seen as a conservative, Fr Bede became, for Fr Edmund and later Fr Paul, 'an ally in a thousand'. As procurator, Fr Bede found the money for the expansion of the school in the late 1920s.[40]

There would also appear to have been conservatism regarding the school, particularly on the part of many of the monks engaged in work on the parishes of the Ampleforth missions.

---

[38] *Ampleforth Journal*, 17/1 (1912). Jubilee Address by Bishop Hedley, pp. 2–13; 'The Ideal of Catholic Education', pp. 25–35; 'Liberty and Responsibility for Boys', pp. 37–43.

[39] Fr Bede's tenure as procurator, the monastic equivalent of a bursar, is given by Fr Paul Nevill in his 'Modern Ampleforth', in McCann and Cary-Elwes, *Ampleforth*, p. 244.

[40] Cary-Elwes, untitled biography of Fr Paul Nevill, version 1, p. 79.

The school that had produced them, and men like Bishop Hedley, whatever his subsequent enthusiasm for change, did not seem too bad a school, especially when the changes being proposed would have brought Ampleforth more into line with Protestant schools. This sort of thinking would be described by a product of the changed Ampleforth such as Fr Columba Cary-Elwes as complacency and led him to comment at the turn of the century that 'few realized the deficiency [of Ampleforth]. There was a false air of learning.'[41] Fr Paul Nevill tended to associate this reluctance to move on from established ways of conducting the school with the conservatism and backwardness of Lancashire Catholicism on which the community and school was principally based. This can be glimpsed in his comment on the Prefect of Discipline appointed in 1904, Fr Joseph Dawson:

> He was not in the least academically minded and, although an exceptionally good man of Lancashire stock, he had few ideas about education or boys' psychology ... he had a rather rigid mind; he believed that every moment of a boy's day had to be planned and so gave them very little of the liberty which would ultimately turn them into responsible creatures.[42]

Most serious of all the objections raised to the reform of the school on public school lines was the change that would be brought about in the relationship between school and monastery. The monastery had always dominated the school. In many respects the school was part of the monastery. While the school had from early on included lay boys, it was still the place that formed members of the community. Before Fr Edmund Matthews built up the Sixth Form just before the Great War, most lay boys left at fifteen or sixteen. Those who stayed on remained because they intended to pursue a monastic vocation. A school of two hundred plus, organized into houses, intended to imitate the Anglican public schools and which, if it were to compete successfully in the gaining of entrance

---

[41]   *Ibid.*, p. 19.
[42]   Fr P Nevill, 'Modern Ampleforth', in McCann and Cary-Elwes, *Ampleforth*, p. 248.

awards at Oxford and Cambridge, would probably need the introduction of well-qualified lay masters, would throw the balance of Ampleforth. It seems reasonable to surmise that the view of those opposed to the growth and transformation of the school was that the school should feed into, and be subordinate to, an Ampleforth focused on the monastic life and the serving of the mission parishes. A growing English public school on the site at Ampleforth might distract the community from this. Housemasterships and the affairs of the school might, moreover, seem of greater importance than monastic life and service in the parishes. It is interesting to note that Fr Placid Dolan, an ally of Fr Edmund and Fr Paul when it came to raising the academic calibre of the school, was an opponent of the plan to expand the school and adopt the house system. According to Fr Columba,

> It was at this point that some of the other Progressives in the community did not follow Fr Paul. Fr Placid Dolan, one of the real pioneers, and with a brain and character well-fitted to cope with the rise of Ampleforth, took the view that such expansion would be detrimental to Ampleforth ... He was against an increase in size, the diluting, as he would call it, of the Ampleforth monastic spirit.[43]

These would seem to have been the issues on which Prior Burge foundered, which caused so much anxiety to Fr Paul Nevill and which led to the cautious approach of Fr Edmund Matthews as headmaster.

It is interesting to note the extent to which these divisions amongst the Ampleforth community were reflected, and to a much greater extent, at Downside some decades later. The comparable figure to Fr Placid at Downside was Dom David Knowles. According to his contemporary as a Downside pupil, the writer Douglas Woodruff, 'his view of the monastic school was that if a man was content to teach boys in a school, that was good and useful work, but it was not what the monastic

---

[43]   Cary-Elwes, untitled biography of Fr Paul Nevill, version 1, p. 79.

life was about'.[44] In 1933 a group of young monks, whose most prominent member was Knowles, proposed setting up a new community where the running of a school would not distract from the monastic life. The scheme was rejected by Rome in 1934 and all but Knowles remained within the Downside community. He went on, as an exclaustrated monk, to become a Fellow of Peterhouse and Regius Professor of History at Cambridge.[45] Whatever the misgivings of Fr Placid and others at Ampleforth, nothing quite so dramatic happened there. Fr Edmund Matthews was able to get on with the development of the school along the lines advocated by Fr Paul and others of what Fr Columba called 'the Progressives'.

That Fr Edmund should have been made headmaster by Abbot Oswald Smith and given the opportunity to lay the foundations on which Fr Paul Nevill was to build is something of a surprise. Fr Oswald had been elected as prior when there was a reaction within the community against the direction the school was taking under Prior Anselm Burge. According to Fr Paul Nevill, 'Fr Oswald had been one of the greatest opponents of his [Prior Burge's] regime, certainly in its early stages'.[46] One of Fr Oswald's first acts as prior had been to reorganize the staffing of the school. Fr Clement Standish, who had been a close associate of Prior Anselm Burge and who had been the prefect in charge of the school, was replaced. In the new order, Fr William Darby had overall control of the school, with the freshly coined title of rector, while Fr Austin Hind became Prefect of Studies and Fr Anselm Turner Prefect of Discipline.[47]

---

44   Douglas Woodruff, obituary of Dom David Knowles in *The Tablet*, 7 December 1974.
45   C. N. L. Brooke, *Oxford Dictionary of National Biography*, http://www. oxforddnb.com/templates/article.jsp?articeid=31322&back. The young monks who shared Knowles's reservations about the influence of the school on monastic life but stayed at Downside would have been senior members of the community in the 1960s when an Ampleforth shaped by Fr Paul Nevill and whose community was solidly behind the school eclipsed Downside as the leading Catholic public school.
46   Fr P. Nevill, 'Modern Ampleforth', in McCann and Cary-Elwes, *Ampleforth*, p. 241.
47   *Ibid.*, p. 243.

This new regime did not see the school prosper. By 1903 the fortunes of Ampleforth College were at a low point. Fr Cuthbert Almond had been able to write a centenary history of Ampleforth, which showed Ampleforth to have peaked coming into the twentieth century. While this may have been true for the monastic community, recently raised to abbey status, it was not true of the school. The successes achieved by the school since the mid-nineteenth century recovery under Fr Wilfrid Cooper seemed in danger of being lost. In 1903, the numbers had dropped to 78 and no boy in the school passed a public examination.[48] Abbot Oswald Smith may have been reluctant to see Ampleforth College turned into an English public school, and may have been opposed to its rapid and excessive expansion, but he could not allow the school to close. The continued prosperity of the school was important to the community. In a world in which Downside was becoming more like a contemporary Anglican public school and similar changes were being effected at Stonyhurst and Beaumont, Ampleforth was in danger of falling out of favour with Catholic parents able to afford boarding school education for their sons. Keeping Ampleforth entirely as it had been before the days of Prior Burge was no longer an option. In these circumstances, Abbot Oswald Smith had to call on Fr Edmund Matthews, the first of the community to benefit from Prior Burge's policy of sending bright young monks to Oxford, and bring him back from Belmont, where he had been teaching novices, to take over the school. Fr Edmund Matthews took charge of the school with the new title of headmaster, a significant step in Ampleforth's structures starting to correspond with those of the wider public school world.

A most valuable insight to Ampleforth during the first part of Fr Edmund Matthews's time as headmaster is provided by an unpublished memoir written by Brigadier N. J. Chamberlain, who was one of the boys who lived through the beginning of Ampleforth's transformation, and who became the College's first head monitor in 1912.

---

[48] Cary-Elwes, untitled biography of Fr Paul Nevill, version 1, p. 66.

When I went to Ampleforth (in 1906), it was a small school of about 130 boys. This was not its only shortcoming. There were only three lay masters, including the part time Arts Master, the Music Master and the Science Master. The remainder of the teaching was done by monks, few of whom had adequate qualifications. Another shortcoming was that the ages of the boys ranged from 10 to 18. In point of fact most boys left when they were 17 or even 16, so, when I went there in 1906 Ampleforth had no Sixth Form in the true sense.[49]

Fr Edmund oversaw a recovery in numbers, the establishment of a genuine Sixth Form which worked to high standards of scholarship and created a climate in which further change was possible. It was under Fr Edmund that the issues relating to Ampleforth's future, and the possibility of it being modelled on the leading Anglican public schools were aired. As Chamberlain commented,

He became Headmaster when Ampleforth was a small, badly taught and unknown school. By the time he died, it had become a large, well taught and well known school. To him must be given the credit for this great achievement.[50]

An indication of the swift impact made by Fr Edmund on his appointment as headmaster is provided by the copies of the course of studies in the Ampleforth Abbey archives. Fr Austin Hind made copies of the course of studies for 1897–8, 1898–9, 1899–1900, 1900–1 and 1903. Before 1903 these are written in exercise books and give a fairly cursory outline of the studies in each subject for each class. In 1903 there is a marked change in the presentation and organization of the course of studies. The whole document is more business-like and professional. It is longer and starts with an index by subject, with page numbers given for the details of the delivery of specific subjects. The old class names, traditional in Catholic colleges, of Lower Syntax, Upper Syntax, Poetry and the rest were omitted and

---

[49]   Chamberlain, untitled memoir, p. 18.
[50]   *Ibid.*

classes were listed as Preparatory Class, First Form, Second Form, Lower Third Form, Higher Third Form, Fourth Form, Fifth Form and Sixth Form. For each form, the subjects to be covered were given prescribed texts with their publishers, prices, and the specific parts of the text to be studied.[51]

The success of Fr Edmund's regime can be seen in the recovery of school numbers. In 1919 the College had, according to Fr Columba Cary-Elwes, 200 pupils.[52] The rise in the standard of scholarship was seen in the College beginning to compete successfully for awards at Oxford. Oxford-educated monastic teachers such as Fr Paul, a historian, and Fr Placid Dolan, a mathematician, set an example for their fellow monk teachers to follow gave directly of their expertise to the boys. Ampleforth had sent a few boys as commoners to Oxford once the prohibition on Catholics attending the ancient universities was lifted, but in 1912, began to win scholarships. Vincent Nasey won an open scholarship in history at Trinity in 1912. In 1913 he was joined at Oxford by Noel Chamberlain, who had been awarded a history scholarship at University College, and Bernard Berge, who had gained a scholarship at Merton.[53]

Outside the academic curriculum, the major changes associated with Fr Edmund were a departure from having discipline exclusively in the hands of monk prefects by the introduction of monitors and replacing association football as the principal winter game with rugby. Rugby was to become of some importance in Ampleforth's rise to the leading rank of public schools, but the more immediately significant change was the introduction of monitors. For the first time at Ampleforth, boys were involved in the disciplining of other boys. The first head monitor and captain of Rugby, Chamberlain, remembered how this change had worked in practice:

> There was no bullying at Ampleforth in my time. Until the monitorial system was belatedly introduced, discipline

---

[51] Ampleforth Abbey Archives, BX51–5.
[52] Cary-Elwes, untitled biography of Fr Paul Nevill, version 1, p. 66. See also footnote 38. There is a discrepancy in the sources for numbers at Ampleforth at this time.
[53] Chamberlain, untitled memoir, p. 19.

was maintained by three monk prefects, but of these only the first prefect really counted. There was corporal punishment. Usually it was not excessive but occasionally, in my opinion, it was . . . In my last year at Ampleforth the conventional British system of boy prefects or monitors was introduced. I was Ampleforth's first Head Monitor, and I did my best to do my job humanely and sensibly. No boy was beaten in my first term as Head Monitor. Discipline was not so good in my second term, so we had to make an example of the worst offender, rather a big boy who ignored the orders of a monitor given in the presence of some small boys. He took his punishment very well and showed no ill feeling towards us.[54]

Fr Edmund's Ampleforth was a successful school, but, notwithstanding his emphasis on higher academic standards, some organizational change and admission to the HMC, it was still more recognizable as a Catholic college than a classic English public school. The school was full at around 200 boys, lacked the house system characteristic of the leading public schools, and was still staffed almost exclusively by members of the monastic community. Moreover, Ampleforth was still not widely recognized as the leading Catholic school. In some important quarters there was recognition of what was being achieved under Fr Edmund. To the end of his life Fr Paul Nevill kept a letter which had been sent to him in 1916 in which the then Cardinal Archbishop of Westminster, Francis Bourne, was reported as saying to a visiting American bishop when asked to name the leading Catholic college in England, 'I think we must look to Ampleforth for the lead. They have quite the finest staff of any of our schools.'[55] From the perspective of numbers and public profile, however, Ampleforth still lagged behind Stonyhurst and (to a lesser extent with regard to numbers) Downside. In 1900, according to Bamford, Ampleforth had 63 pupils; in 1919, 170. The comparable figures for Stonyhurst were 200 and 333; for Downside, 66 and 190.[56]

---

54   *Ibid.*, pp. 13–14.
55   Cary-Elwes, untitled biography of Fr Paul Nevill, version 1, p. 92.
56   T. W. Bamford, *Public School Data: A Compilation of Data on Public and Related Schools (Boys) Mainly from 1866.* Aids to Research in Education

Of the three schools it was Downside that was furthest down the road of assimilating the structures and ethos of the leading public schools. The school at Downside, under Fr Edmund's counterpart Dom Leander Ramsay, headmaster from 1902 to 1918, also began to transform. As Dom Hubert van Zeller wrote in his history of Downside,

> During his sixteen years of office . . . Dom Leander more than doubled the size of the school, built extensively, shaped the system of authority amongst the boys, broadened the academic horizons, gave the greatest encouragement to games, founded the corps and exercised a remarkable influence in the religious and spiritual life of the school.[57]

As with the reformers at Ampleforth, Ramsay had to push through policies in the school that broke with earlier tradition and, as at Ampleforth, these changes were not entirely met with approval by the older generation. The last Prefect of Studies at Downside was Dom Wulstan Pearson; van Zeller observes of him:

> For years Dom Wulstan Pearson had held the reins of discipline in his own two hands and he was convinced that to give a boy authority was to invite either slackness or injustice . . . He became increasingly puzzled at the emergence of what was clearly the beginnings of a great school from the chrysalis with which he had been so long familiar.

Van Zeller followed this with the judgment of an Old Gregorian, the product of Ramsay's school, on Dom, later Bishop, Pearson:

> I can well believe that he was a good bishop and a good monk . . . but I do not think he was a good schoolmaster. What was good enough for his fathers was good enough

No. 2 (Hull: University of Hull, 1974), p. 11. Figures taken from Table 3; see also footnote 19. The figure given by Fr Columba Cary-Elwes for Ampleforth in 1919 is 200. These figures cannot be reconciled. They give, however, a broad indication of the numbers in the school.
[57]   van Zeller, *Downside*, p. 90.

for him. He was entirely against rugger, the OTC, hot
water, comfort, trusting boys and any form of amenity.[58]

It was Fr Paul Nevill, backed by Fr Edmund as abbot, who
made the same sort of changes effected by Fr Leander Ramsay
at Downside and, if anything, took them even further. By
the time of Fr Paul's death in 1954 Ampleforth was a leading
public school and, notwithstanding the claims of Downside
and Stonyhurst, the leading Catholic school of this type. In
analysing how this was brought about, it is useful to under-
stand the essential continuity that lay at the heart of Fr Paul
Nevill's vision for the school. An appreciation of this puts his
theoretical writings, his frustrations with the slow pace of
change and the energy with which he forced through change,
when given his opportunity as headmaster, into context.

Fundamentally, Fr Paul was convinced of the compatibility of Catholicism with an intense English patriotism. As Fr
Columba Cary-Elwes wrote of him,

> He was so intensely English that he wanted to show that
> English Catholics were as public-spirited and as capable
> as any other section of the community. His aim was to
> bring back Catholics into the stream of the nation's life
> after four hundred years of isolation.[59]

In this, however, a crucial mechanism was to be the development of separate Catholic schools, particularly Ampleforth.
This approach fits in with the irony and paradox discerned
by Parsons and others in studies that show the Catholic community, from the later nineteenth century, integrating into a
wider society while still operating within its own exclusive
institutions.[60] It is much the same with Fr Paul Nevill and his
associates. They wanted to assert their Englishness and to
take a full role in what they perceived as their proper place
in English society, but this had to be done as Catholics and
through Catholic schools.

---

[58] *Ibid.*, p. 67.
[59] Cary-Elwes, untitled biography of Fr Paul Nevill, version 1, p. 173.
[60] *Ibid.*, p.79.

Fr Paul's own background gave an edge to the intensity with which he held his views about the issues facing the English Catholic Church and the means of their resolution. The Nevills were an old Catholic gentry family with southern roots. Fr Paul's branch of the family was in straitened circumstances. When the time came for decisions on the schooling of her sons, Mrs Nevill was advised by the Downside monk, Dom Ephrem Guy, in whose Suffolk parish the family then lived, to send them to Ampleforth where the fees were lower than at Downside. Valentine Nevill, as he was before entering the community with the religious name of Paul, therefore, found himself in 1891 in a small northern school, most of whose pupils came from the Lancashire parishes served by the Ampleforth community.[61] The school had long since ceased to be patronized by the Catholic aristocracy. The Ampleforth of the 1890s could be seen as very much part of a provincial Catholic ghetto.

This chafed with the young Valentine Nevill. Writing of Fr Paul's time as a schoolboy, Fr Columba noted that

> Lancashire at this time was the chief centre of the Catholic population. They were solid, unimaginative as well as uninterested, in matters beyond the boundaries of the Ribble Valley. Their pronunciation was different from the southern modulation of the Nevill brothers and a few others. Even to this day there are men who find it hard to think kindly of Val Nevill of schoolboy days, he so teased them for their provincial accent and provincial outlook too.[62]

Fr Columba's view, in summary, was that Fr Paul 'belonged to the old recusant families; he went to school in a tiny school whose outlook was backward, somewhat foreign—from having been in exile for so many years—extremely conservative and anti-Protestant, in some ways ultra rigid'.[63] Fr Paul would not have an Ampleforth that was provincial and isolated. The intensity and persistence with which he held this view can

---

[61] *Ibid.*, p. 13.
[62] *Ibid.*, p. 25.
[63] *Ibid.*, p. 9.

be seen in an exchange when Fr Paul was well into his time as headmaster. In 1930 he was a member of an HMC party that toured Canada. It was put to him by the Warden of Hart House, part of the University of Toronto, that Ampleforth, as a Catholic school, differed from 'the ordinary English public school'. This was Fr Paul's response:

> Come and stay at Ampleforth. We are English. My ancestors fought for King Charles. They have fought for England in every war for the last three centuries. We are not organized on continental lines at Ampleforth . . . my boys may be Roman Catholics but they are English. They go to Oxford. There are ten now at the House, your own college; intellectually, athletically, morally, they are as good as any men there.[64]

Towards the end of his life in correspondence with a former pupil Fr Paul again pursued the theme of the compatibility of Catholicism with Englishness:

> The Anglican establishment and Protestantism are not real forces. They battened on anti-Roman propaganda. That is what keeps them alive — the idea that Catholicism is a 'dago' religion and no Catholic is capable or indeed allowed to think for himself.[65]

Fr Paul had latched on to a notion of Englishness based on the manliness, integrity and independence, which the Protestant public schools sought to inculcate. The things that made Catholicism disliked in England, such as the possibility of divided loyalty between Church and State, a Church which sought to control rigidly its adherents, showy displays in religious practice and an unthinking obedience to the clergy, were seen by Fr Paul as not inherent in Catholicism, but imports from the continent. If English Catholics were to take a full place in English society, they would have to abandon practices picked up from continental Catholicism and emphasize Eng-

---

[64] *Ibid.*, p. 206. The original note supplied by Bickersteth of his memories of Fr Paul is also in the archive.

[65] Ampleforth Abbey Archives, BX05 03 7M12, Letter from Fr P. Nevill to Basil Rooke Ley, 30 December 1951.

lish traditions. This obsession with Englishness and patriotism also helps explain the importance accorded to military service within the Catholic schools intent on becoming leading English public schools. Sending boys into the forces was a clear demonstration of patriotism and of the success of the Catholic schools in fulfilling one of the fundamental aims of the public schools: producing leaders of men.[66] This, then, provides the perspective from which to look at the ideological debates in which Fr Paul participated during the years before the Great War, and the way in which Ampleforth was re-structured and its fortunes, from the viewpoint of its standing in the English public school world, so dramatically improved after 1924.

In the period in which the debates about Ampleforth's future were thrashed out, 1912 was a key year. The *Ampleforth Journal* of 1912 reported on the celebrations of the fiftieth anniversary of the opening of Fr Wilfrid Cooper's new school building in 1861. The centrepiece of this was an address by the Amplefordian bishop of Newport, Bishop Hedley. Bishop Hedley had been a prime mover in securing permission for Catholics to attend Oxford and Cambridge. He was keen that his school should be in a position to take advantage of this. In the words of his biographer,

> He did not undervalue that excellent but unfinished education which our Catholic colleges gave ... but he was not willing that our Catholic youth should remain content with means so scanty and so far removed from the attainment of complete and finished scholarship.[67]

In his address, Bishop Hedley endorsed the ideas that radicals such as Fr Paul had been pushing within the school and community:

> For real education there must be that continuous skilful guiding and piloting, without pushing or forcing, which makes a boy turn his acquirements into mental growth,

---

[66] See pp. 20–1 above for the success of Ampleforth and Downside in sending boys to Sandhurst.
[67] J. A. Wilson, *Life of Bishop Hedley* (London: Burns and Oates, 193), p. 227.

and discipline his own mind heart and soul. To achieve such a result in a school, first, the boys must be left judiciously to themselves, secondly the masters must forbear from taking too much notice of them; thirdly, the brilliant boys must not be made too much of, and the average ones must never be neglected; and lastly, cramming and feverish work for examinations should be carefully kept down, for work of that kind runs off mind and character like a shower of rain from the roof.[68]

Alongside the bishop's address were two articles by Fr Edmund and Fr Paul. Fr Edmund wrote on 'The Ideal of Catholic Education', and Fr Paul on 'Liberty and Responsibility for Boys'. Fr Edmund reminded parents of the importance of a Catholic education:

> If, then, there is this Catholic atmosphere of religious truth and moral virtue, those parents take on themselves a grave responsibility who neglect to avail themselves of it, and who put their children in a non-Catholic atmosphere in their school life. If ever there was any force in their plea of the importance of social caste, it has grown weaker as the Catholic schools have developed, and, moreover, there is no benefit that can outweigh the good of a Catholic environment.

He went on to acknowledge the growing demand for a public school type of education to be made available in Catholic schools and to argue that this was being achieved, without damage to Catholic educational traditions.

> Some parents would urge that they are anxious to secure the 'public school' type of education for their boys, the manly independence and sense of responsibility that is associated with the name of Arnold of Rugby and the system that he has made popular. It is true that our old Catholic schools did inherit something of the Continental system of supervision; they regard the boys sometimes with the eye of a foreign 'professor', they preserved a touch of the ecclesiastical type of school that went back beyond the Continental system

---

[68]   *Ampleforth Journal*, 17/1 (1912), p. 13.

to the mediaeval schools of our own country. This system, however, has been gradually modified. In most Catholic schools the upper boys are given their share of responsibility, the supervision of masters is giving way to supervision by boys, and now that many of our Catholic parents are coming to recognize the necessity of keeping their boys at school until their eighteenth year, this system will more and more obtain, since the upper boys will be of an age to use their power with moderation and prudence. At the same time there will always be in a Catholic school that venerates tradition, a limited supervision on the part of the master arising not from an un-English distrust of the boy, but from a feeling of responsibility in those who stand 'to boys, a responsibility which recognizes that one may pay too dearly for unlimited liberty.[69]

Fr Paul went beyond Fr Edmund and justified the full-scale switch to the house system:

It is now generally realized that English Catholic boys cannot be brought up on a system that is really continental in origin and in spirit. Still more important is the fact that Catholics are no longer regarded as pariahs by their fellow countrymen, that they now find their way as a matter of course to the universities, into the army and the civil service and are daily called upon to take up important positions and fill important posts ... By liberty is meant that in the out of school hours there is no immediate supervision of boys by masters. No master watches over them in their playing hours, but they are left to themselves, bound by few and necessary rules, which ought to become less in number as they grow older, and the observance of which is made a matter of personal honour and trust among the boys themselves ... The evils that supervision attempts to meet would be largely met by the adoption in our Catholic schools of the House System. The main difficulties of boarding schools come from the herding of boys, or the barrack

system, and this is best remedied by the adoption of
the House System, which gives all the advantages of
a big school, and allows for the play of all those good
influences which come from a small school.[70]

He went on to say that 'The best argument for the argument
here advocated is the sense of mutual distrust and the con-
sequent habit of evasion which the system of supervision
breeds'.[71] This 1912 article by Fr Paul represented a blueprint
for a change in the structure of the school that would in turn
lead to a changed ethos. The house system alone, however,
while fundamental, was not all that was required.

Fr Paul's transformation of Ampleforth into the Catholic
school most closely resembling the leading Anglican schools,
taking his school into the upper reaches of this world, is fairly
straightforward. Under Fr Paul, Ampleforth acquired a fully
developed house system. The atmosphere in which the school
was conducted, as laid out in the 1912 article, became one
in which greater responsibility was devolved to boys. There
was an increasing adoption of the games cult pervasive in the
contemporary public school world and, more importantly, the
academic standing of the school was further increased by the
appointment of highly qualified and effective lay masters.
These changes saw the school increase in numbers to over 400
by the time of Fr Paul's death and Ampleforth was once again
the most fashionable of the Catholic schools. The attractiveness
of Ampleforth to the Catholic aristocracy and gentry can be
seen in the list reeled off by Bence-Jones in a recent study of
the grander of the Catholic families. He pointed out that

> Father Paul's pupils included Miles and Michael Fitzalan-
> Howard and their two younger brothers, the sons of Lord
> Howard of Glossop and Baroness Beaumont; Peter Kerr
> who became the twelfth Marquis of Lothian, and his
> brother and the three sons of the fifth Marquis of Bute
> and their Bertie cousins.

[70]   *Ibid.*, p. 38.
[71]   *Ibid.*, p. 39.

He went on to include the fourteenth Lord Stafford and several Frasers, Stirlings and Constable Maxwells.[72] This time,
however, the Catholic gentry and aristocracy were much less
isolated than they had been in the days of Fr Augustine Baines.
This connection with the aristocracy and gentry helped give
Ampleforth a national reputation.

Fr Paul took the major step of organizing Ampleforth under
the house system in 1926. Within the old central building,
erected around the original house of Fr Anselm Bolton and
the connected school building put up by Fr Wilfrid Cooper,
there were three internal houses: St Bede's, St Aidan's and St
Oswald's. St Cuthbert's was built as an external house. By the
1930s Fr Paul had decided that the school should continue to
grow. In 1932 he told the Abbot's Council that

> I have sought much advice from Headmasters elsewhere
> about the best number for a school, and the advisers in
> whom I have most faith have named 400 to 450, we at
> present have a little over 200 boys of public school age.[73]

This development also saw the expansion of Ampleforth's
provision of preparatory school education. In the early stages
of the College's reform a decision had been taken by the community in 1913 to have a preparatory school for boys under
fourteen years of age. Sites at Malvern and Oxford were considered but a Lower School, later known as Junior House, was
opened in 1916 at Ampleforth. Fr Paul's expansion drive of the
1930s involved the creation of a second preparatory school.
Gilling Castle was acquired by Ampleforth in 1929 and the first
boys moved in in 1930. It is interesting that even at this date
there was some resistance in the community to the expansion
of the College. The Chapter of 1929 rejected Abbot Matthews's
original proposal to buy Gilling Castle. There was concern
over the financial risk but also the objection that the growth of
the school was absorbing too many monks; taking them away
from the parishes and community life. Abbot Matthews had

---

72   Bence-Jones, *Catholic Families*, p .307.
73   Cary-Elwes, untitled biography of Fr Paul Nevill, version 1, p. 108.

101

to secure consent for the Gilling project by calling an extraordinary chapter.[74]

Between 1933 and 1935 three new houses in the College were created. Fr Paul told Chapter in 1935 that this should 'make the school sufficiently large to enable us to compete intellectually and in all other respects with the best Public Schools in the country'.[75] St Dunstan's was an internal house and two more external houses were built and opened as St Wilfrid's and St Edward's. Alongside the building of houses was the expansion of the school's teaching accommodation. Between 1926 and 1936 a quadrangle was completed housing science laboratories, classrooms, a school shop and rooms for the headmaster.[76] Fr Paul had little difficulty in finding Catholic parents to support this expansion of the school. When Fr William Price took over as headmaster, one of his more pressing problems was how to cope with the demand for places at Ampleforth.[77]

The house system at Ampleforth was taken further than at any Catholic school; as Evennett remarked in his correspondence with Fr Paul, 'your house system seems to me to be the only real fully developed house system in any Catholic school'.[78] At Ampleforth, as in the leading Anglican public schools, housemasters were given considerable autonomy and allowed to correspond directly with parents.[79] Fr Paul

[74]   Details of the decision to engage in preparatory school education are given in Marrett-Crosby, *Ampleforth*, p. 69. The decision to purchase Gilling Castle is covered on p. 71.
[75]   Cary-Elwes, untitled biography of Fr Paul Nevill, version 1, p. 108.
[76]   For details of the expansion of the campus at Ampleforth see P. Nevill in McCann and Cary-Elwes, *Ampleforth*, pp. 258–9.
[77]   Ampleforth Abbey Archives, HX 92–20, Memorandum from Fr William Price, December 1955 on numbers in the school. Fr William proposed to reserve 10 per cent of places for relatives of the community and sons of old boys, to maintain current fees and to raise the Common Entrance pass mark by 20 per cent over the next three years.
[78]   Ampleforth Abbey Archives, DX65, Letter from H. O. Evennett to Fr P. Nevill, 15 September 1943.
[79]   In his study of the part played by public schools in nineteenth-century Britain, Joyce remarks upon an extraordinarily decentralized and *laissez-faire* way of doing things. He sees the correspondence

was keen that Ampleforth's houses should reflect the different characters of the monk housemaster placed in charge of them. As he trusted boys, so he was prepared to trust such valued monastic colleagues as Fr Stephen Marwood to exercise their own judgment in the running of their houses. The building of houses separate from the main school building was also a departure from Catholic tradition. Stonyhurst and the Jesuits schools housed their pupils within a single building. Downside adopted the house system, but accommodated all of its boys in the same central building.

Concomitant with the introduction of the house system for Fr Paul was revision of the school rules. Fr Paul was well known for dislike of rules and the over-regulation which he saw as endemic in the pre-1924 Ampleforth. He was recorded as saying:

> I am quite certain that the fewer rules and regulations we can have the better and the more we can conduct our schools on the principles of a small and well-conducted home the more chance there is of boys acquiring self-discipline.[80]

One of Fr Paul's first acts as headmaster was to scrap the old rules. Looking at the sets of school rules in the Ampleforth archives (those for 1822, signed by Prior Burgess, 1908, drawn up by Fr Edmund Matthews and 1926, Fr Paul Nevill's version, survive) the change made by Fr Paul is not as dramatic as might be supposed from a reading of his views on rules for boys in general and the old school rules of Ampleforth in particular. Examining rules on paper, of course, does not tell the extent to which, or the spirit in which, they were implemented. On the written page, however, there is some continuity between Fr Edmund's and Fr Paul's rules. The 1908 rules start with provisions for the religious observance of the boys, commencing with their morning offering, running through

between housemasters and parents as at the centre of governance, highlighting J. B. Oldham, a housemaster at Shrewsbury, said to have written 3,000 letters a year to parents and old boys. Joyce, *The State of Freedom*, p. 269.

[80] Cary-Elwes, untitled biography of Fr Paul Nevill, version 1, p. 137.

arrangements for daily Mass and finishing with guidelines for the examination of conscience at night. The 1926 rules are virtually the same in this respect. When it comes to matters of more general school order and routine, there are still considerable similarities. Both sets of rules say how boys should conduct themselves on rising and how to proceed about the school. Both insist that the Study should be a place of silence. Even after Fr Paul became headmaster, his interpretation of liberty and responsibility for boys left Ampleforth a tightly structured place. One clear difference between the school rules of 1908 and 1926, however, was in the justification for the respectful treatment of, and obedience towards, masters. The 1908 rules followed those of 1822, in that 'The boys should always consider their masters as holding the place of Almighty God in their regard and as such revere them'.[81] In 1926 this had changed to 'He should remember that his masters stand in the place of his parents so should try to obey them less from fear of punishment than from a true spirit of subjugation and good will'.[82]

The crucial difference in the rules, however, was the role played by the newly installed housemasters and the boy monitors in disciplinary procedures.[83] In 1908 discipline was very much in the hands of the Prefect. Only the prefect could administer corporal punishment.[84] In 1926,

> Corporal punishment is administered in exceptional cases by the Headmaster and as a normal rule by the Housemasters. The Head Monitor of the School may administer corporal punishment with the permission of the Housemaster to whose house the offender belongs.

---

[81] Ampleforth Abbey Archives, BX51–1, 1908 School Rules, p. 23. See above for a similar point in the 1822 rules.

[82] Ampleforth Abbey Archives, BX51–3, 1926 School Rules, item 8.

[83] 'Monitor' was the term used by Fr Edmund when he created a head pupil supported by other boys with some authority in 1912. Fr Paul kept to 'monitor' for boys with school-wide authority but in the 1926 rules 'prefect' was employed for those whose writ only ran within a house.

[84] Ampleforth Abbey Archives, BX51–1, 1908 School Rules, p. 29.

The same rule applies to the Head Monitors of the houses
in the case of members of their own house.[85]

The 1926 rules also list a substantial number of areas in which
school monitors and house prefects were to be involved in the
enforcement of rules. It was the responsibility of school monitors, for example, to maintain silence in the Study and in the
Library.[86] In return there were specified privileges for monitors
and senior boys. Monitors were allowed to receive food par-
cels from home without permission from their housemaster.[87]

With regard to teaching, under Fr Paul Ampleforth saw the
efforts of the monks substantially aided by laymen. In 1944,
when Evennett wrote about Catholic schools, Ampleforth had
a teaching staff of thirty-seven monks and twenty-two laymen.[88]
All the housemasters were monks: monks oversaw most of the
games and undertook the majority of teaching. At the top end
of the school, however, much of the Sixth Form and scholarship
teaching was the work of lay masters. Classics was strengthened initially by the recruitment of Mr Bamford in 1927, who
later left to become the senior master in Classics at Dulwich.
Walter Shrewring came a year later and remained for the rest
of his long and distinguished career. Thomas Charles-Edwards
was taken onto to the staff to teach history. He too remained at
Ampleforth throughout his career and did much to produce
the string of open awards in history at Oxford and Cambridge
that were so important to the increasing standing of the school.[89]

Games represent the one area in which Fr Paul was not
entirely enthusiastic about English public schools. According to Fr Columba, 'Fr Paul never fell for that later idolizing
of games which overtook the public schools in the second

---

[85] Ampleforth Abbey Archives, BX51–3, 1926 School Rules, item 8. As
      described in the memoir of Fr Edmund's first head monitor, corporal
      punishment administered by a boy was possible before Fr Paul's
      headmastership, but the 1926 Rules represent a substantial extension
      of the scope for senior boys to chastize fellow pupils.
[86] *Ibid.*, item 3.
[87] *Ibid.*, item 7.
[88] Evennett, *The Catholic Schools*, p. 86.
[89] Fr Paul's most significant lay teaching appointments are listed in A.
      Marett-Crosby, *Ampleforth*, p. 113.

and third decades of this century'.[90] The research of Mangan
indicates that issue could be taken with Fr Columba over the
timing of the English public school obsession with games.
The cult of athleticism had begun to flourish well before the
twentieth century.[91] Fr Columba was correct, however, when
it came to Fr Paul's views. In private correspondence with an
old boy, Fr Paul bridled at the suggestion that Ampleforth's
standing and full entry list were due in large part to the successes of its elevens and fifteens. He believed that Ampleforth's
success had much more to do with its academic results and
the character of its boys, and commented that

> I only want the boys to be capable of holding their own
> athletically and ready to show the best spirit in all games.
> Then I am happy. I don't think that it is good for them
> to win all their games. They lose their sense of values.
> We have just won seven open awards to Oxford and
> Cambridge and I hope to win more before the academic
> year comes to an end.[92]

Something similar can be found at Stonyhurst. Stonyhurst
was one of the schools focused upon by Mangan in his study
of the public schools and the cult of athleticism. In his view,
Stonyhurst stood out from the Anglican schools in its approach
to games:

> From the first moments and for the best part of eighty
> years Stonyhurst was characterized by a considerable
> cultural, geographical, religious and educational
> distance from mainstream public school life. This fact
> requires emphasis because it was the major reason for
> the idiosyncratic nature of the school and for its rejection
> of both the animus and emblems of athleticism.[93]

In Mangan's view, Stonyhurst had not entirely lost this distinctive approach to games by the time of the Great War. For him,

---

[90] Cary-Elwes, untitled biography of Fr Paul Nevill, version 1, p. 23.
[91] See Mangan, *Athleticism*.
[92] Ampleforth Abbey Archives, BX05–03 7MI2, Letter from Fr Paul
      Nevill to Basil Rooke Ley, 31 December 1952.
[93] Mangan, *Athleticism*, p. 60.

'Both athletic idealism and indulgence were firmly repressed. There, religion was, and was to firmly remain, the source of moral soundness, and the adversary of moral corruption.'[94] Notwithstanding this, however, by the 1890s there was change relating to games at Stonyhurst. According to Mangan, this consisted of 'sporting rituals and symbols of the Protestant public schools but to an extent this was because of the need to gain acceptance as a public school'.[95] Reinforcing the perception of this need were letters from boys in school magazines calling for college colours for games and stressing the importance of successful cricket sides to the school's standing. In 1890 an internal football league was established at Stonyhurst and college colours for the cricket XI, first requested by boys in 1894, were instituted in 1896. The rector of Stonyhurst was not happy with these developments, but as Mangan observed,

> Stonyhurst was a school for upper class boys proud of its upper class status and despite official concern could only carry its individualism so far ... If the symbols and rituals of athleticism were integral to the English public school, then to ignore them completely was to emphasize difference, perpetuate suspicion and prolong the school's history of social insecurity.[96]

In the end, all Catholic schools became adherents of the games cult, especially after their switch to rugby. Whatever the personal views of headmasters such as Fr Paul Nevill, games were of considerable importance to the Catholic schools that sought to advance themselves in the English public school world. Once the emulation of the public school ethos was started, it was difficult to pick and choose elements of it. Many parents, masters and boys were only too happy to embrace the games cult. Catholic schools, as latecomers to the world of the English

---

[94] *Ibid.*, p. 66.
[95] *Ibid.* O'Neill also considers how far Catholic schools in England patronized by the Irish gentry, (especially Stonyhurst) embraced the cult of games. C. O'Neill, *Catholics of Consequence-Transnational Education, Social Mobility and the Irish Catholic Elite, 1850–1900* (Oxford: Oxford University Press, 2014), p. 102.
[96] Mangan, *Athleticism*, p. 164.

public schools, tended to display the zeal of converts when it came to games. As Evennett wrote in 1944,

> There is no doubt that rugger has been a great success from every point of view in the Catholic schools and that their general prestige and repute in public opinion which is perhaps the ultimate arbiter of what is or is not a public school has largely been made by their rugger success on public school fields, at the universities and in first class amateur games.[97]

When it comes to gauging the responsibility for Ampleforth's success as a public school, Fr Paul's contribution has to be placed in context. He was not responsible for the changing climate within the Catholic Church and within the wider English society that made it possible for a Catholic school to make such an advance. What he did in the school was, to a large extent, built on the ground prepared by others and the school was not to reach its zenith in the public school world until after his death. It is hard, however, to envisage Ampleforth reaching its position as 'the Catholic Eton' without him. Coming into the twentieth century Ampleforth was the smallest and least well known of the Catholic colleges that could claim continuous involvement in the education of Catholic boys since penal times. Arguably, it was not even as well placed as the Jesuit foundation of the mid-nineteenth century, Beaumont. Ampleforth, however, by the mid-twentieth century had, along with the other Catholic schools that had achieved HMC status, broken into the public school world. Stonyhurst, Downside and Ampleforth were perceived as being in, or at least not far away from, the top flight of the public school hierarchy. The Benedictine schools, if anything, had the edge over Stonyhurst. This was achieved under Fr Paul. All the Catholic schools, as has been seen, were in the business, to a greater or lesser extent, of integrating themselves into the receptive world of the public schools by cultivating an ethos built on house systems, prefectorial power, and games, and by tailoring their curricula and teaching to the demands of an examination system whose

---

[97] Evennett, *The Catholic Schools*, p. 118.

crowning point was the winning of open awards at Oxford and Cambridge. Ampleforth did so well because Fr Paul was exceptionally good at operating in this environment and realizing his vision for the school. Fr Paul was highly respected by fellow headmasters and educationalists. He was used by the Government as an advisor and in 1936 the HMC held its annual meeting at Ampleforth.[98]

The association between particular headmasters and the rise of public schools is well known. Starting with Arnold at Rugby, the history of the English public school is replete with examples of exceptional headmasters pushing their schools from relative obscurity into the leading ranks: Thring at Uppingham, Percival at Clifton, Cotton at Marlborough, Almond at Loretto, Sanderson at Oundle and so on. That the success of a school should be bound up with the activities of an individual headmaster is quite compatible with modern educational research. A modern survey of research on effective schools by Reynolds and Teddlie has stated, 'We do not know of a study that has not shown that leadership is important within effective schools, with that leadership nearly always being provided by the headteacher'.[99] Fr Paul Nevill has a good claim to be one of those head teachers categorized as a 'transformational leader' by Murphy and Louis and to fit in with the 'case studies showing the importance of individual leaders with mission' considered by Louis and Miles.[100] It is interesting to see how Fr Paul Nevill fits the profile of an outstanding school leader drawn up by Levine and Lezotte. According to them, the outstanding leader possesses eight characteristics:

> Superior Instructional Leadership.
> Support for Teachers.

---

[98] Cary-Elwes, untitled biography of Fr Paul Nevill, version 1, p. 102.

[99] D. Reynolds and C. Teddlie, 'The Process of School Effectiveness', in D. Reynolds and C. Teddlie (eds), *The International Handbook of School Effectiveness* (Brighton: Falmer Press, 2000), p. 141.

[100] See K. S. Louis and M. B. Miles, *Improving the Urban High School* and J. Murphy and K. S. Louis, *Reshaping the Principalship: Insights from Transformational Reform Efforts* as cited in Reynolds and Teddlie, *School Effectiveness*, p. 141.

High Expenditure of Time and Energy for School
Improvement.
Vigorous Selection and Replacement of Teachers.
Maverick Orientation and Buffering.
Frequent Personal Monitoring of School Activities and
Sense Making.
Acquisition of Resources.
Availability and Effective Utilization of Instructional
Support Personnel.[101]

Fr Paul was a well-qualified and skilled teacher himself.
He was sought out by Arnold Toynbee to coach his son for
entrance to Oxford to read history, following the boy's expul-
sion from Rugby in 1934 because of an involvement with
Communism.[102] Fr Paul took great pains in the recruitment
of his staff and was supportive of them. Few men could have
put more time and energy into the running and promotion of
their schools than Fr Paul. Although he left his housemasters
with a considerable degree of autonomy, helping to create to
the 'top-downess and bottom-upness' in school organization
identified as important in the transformation of a school by
Murphy and Louis,[103] he was in touch with everything that
went on in the school. Crucial in this were the formal weekly
housemasters' meetings in his room, reinforced by talking
to staff and boys. Through such means, Fr Paul had plenty
of opportunity to push his vision of what the school should
be about and to monitor how things were progressing. The
prowess of Fr Paul as a leader was identified in the first HMI
report produced on Ampleforth in 1945. The context for this
was discussion of the teaching staff. The Inspectors remarked
upon the academic qualifications of the lay staff at Ampleforth
often being better than those of their monastic colleagues and

---

[101] D. U. Levine and L. W. Lezotte, 'Unusually Effective Schools: A
Review and Analysis of Research and Practice', *School Effectiveness
and School Improvement*, 1/3 (1990). See Table 4.2, Item 1, as cited in
Reynolds and Teddlie, *School Effectiveness*, p. 144.
[102] Ampleforth Abbey Archives, BX05–03 7M12, Correspondence
between Fr Paul and Arnold Toynbee contained in the material for
the projected biography of Fr Paul by Robert Speaight.
[103] Murphy and Louis, cited in Reynolds and Teddlie, *School Effectiveness*.

observed that this did not diminish the monks as teachers, for all were well read and keen to improve: 'The qualities which stand out are frankness, humility, being anxious to learn and above all a selfless devotion to the work to which they have dedicated themselves'. The Inspectors went on:

> Of these the Headmaster is a remarkable example; appointed in 1924 his vision has brought the school into the line of English public school education and he is well known in many quarters of the educational world; his influence on the school is manifest and though it is pervasive it is not dominating for he appears to be a leader among equals by being the servant of all.[104]

That Fr Paul was something of a maverick is also clear. His character was complex. His nickname was 'Posh Paul' and according to Fr Columba, 'Had he wanted he could have posed as a walking Burke's Peerage'.[105] In spite of this concern for family background and social standing, which was not entirely a problem for a headmaster whose vision for the school included attracting the Catholic gentry, there are numerous accounts in the unpublished biography by Fr Columba, and the reminiscences of Fr Paul sent to Fr Columba and Robert Speaight, of Fr Paul's selflessness, humility, generosity and piety. Fr Columba wrote that 'The story of how he showed the chauffeur round Ampleforth while someone else showed round the Marchioness is not an isolated example of his considerateness'.[106] Through the force of his character and energy, Fr Paul was able to realize what he wanted for Ampleforth. He was able to attract the staff to deliver the standard of education he required and he was able to attract the parents whose sons he wanted at Ampleforth.

Much of how Fr Paul was able to exert such influence is now beyond the historian. The impression he made and the reputation he did so much to create for the school was largely achieved by word of mouth. Parents decide to send children to

---

[104] Ampleforth Abbey Archives, GX 87 31 7S 57, HMI Report on Ampleforth, 1945, p. 8.
[105] Cary-Elwes, untitled biography of Fr Paul Nevill, version 1, p. 9.
[106] *Ibid.*, p. 90.

particular schools on the basis of recommendations given by friends and relatives in the course of day-to-day social inter-action. The Ampleforth Abbey archives, however, illustrate how well Fr Paul and his school were thought of in Oxford and how he operated to improve the position of Ampleforth in the vital business of raising its profile in university admissions.

On taking over the school in 1924, Fr Paul had been advised by A. W. Pickard, Chairman of the Oxford and Cambridge Examination Board, to 'Get the studies right, Nevill, and the rest will follow'.[107] Success in achieving scholarships was also something impressed upon Fr Paul by his old tutor and friend, Sir Ernest Barker. In 1931, Sir Ernest wrote:

> I should like to congratulate you on the wonderful success of your school . . . The one thing I want to see is classical and historical scholarships won by your boys as much as by Rugby and Marlborough—And then I do not know what will be left for you to do.[108]

When it came to Oxford admissions and the securing of these scholarships in the late 1920s and 1930s, and in influencing important families to send their sons to Ampleforth, Fr Paul was aided by the support of the Catholic chaplain at Oxford, Fr Ronald Knox. Knox was well placed to know about the public school world and how a school might chart its rise within it. He had been educated at Eton and had taught at Shrewsbury before his conversion to Catholicism. Afterwards, he taught at St Edmund's, Ware, before his appointment to the Catholic chaplaincy at Oxford.[109] From the correspondence between Frs Nevill and Knox, it would appear that Knox favoured Ampleforth amongst the Catholic schools supplying men to the university. Knox appears to have found Amplefordians more congenial than those from Downside. He wrote to Fr Paul in 1926 that 'I'm very glad to feel that I shall have to do with Ampleforth people such a lot; to tell the truth the Down-

---

[107]   *Ibid.*, p. 104.
[108]   *Ibid.*, p. 47.
[109]   Sheridan Gilley, Knox, Ronald Arbuthnot, Roman Catholic Priest and Writer. *Oxford Dictionary of National Biography* http://www.oxforddnb.com/view/printable/34358.

side young men I meet up at Cambridge terrify me a little'.[110]
Fr Knox helped Ampleforth in the recruitment, as a pupil, of
the grandson of the former prime minister, Herbert Asquith.
Socially, the young Asquith was something of a catch. His
mother Katherine, the widow of Asquith's son Raymond, who
had been killed during the Great War, was a Catholic convert.
Asquith expected his grandson, and heir to his Earldom of
Oxford and Asquith, to attend a major public school. Educated
at the City of London School, Asquith had sent his sons to
Winchester College. The boy's mother, however, wanted her
son to have a Catholic education and was advised by Fr Knox
to choose Ampleforth. Fr Knox wrote to Nevill:

> If you are taking the Aponyi boy, do write to Lord
> Oxford and tell him so because Katherine Asquith has
> apparently decided to send her boy to a Catholic school
> and I have just been giving her a violent lecture (not
> for publication) about Ampleforth as compared with
> other Benedictine schools. There is sure to be a furious
> row with the old man, and it might just make it better if
> he's friendly disposed towards Ampleforth at the time.[111]

The presence of Hungarian aristocracy in the school, it seems,
made Ampleforth more acceptable. Whatever the social character of its intake, however, there would have been little cause
for Asquith to be disappointed with the academic outcome
of his daughter-in-law's decision. Succeeding to his grandfather's title as an eleven-year-old in 1928, Julian Asquith left
Ampleforth having won a Balliol scholarship. He went on at
Oxford to take firsts in both classical moderations and *literae
humaniores*, graduating in 1938.[112]

At least part of the reason for Asquith's academic success at
Ampleforth was the recruitment to its staff of Walter Shewring.

---

[110] Ampleforth Abbey Archives, DX65, Fr R. A. Knox to Fr Paul Nevill,
1 July 1926.
[111] *Ibid.* Fr R. A. Knox to Fr P. Nevill, 27 October 1927. The 'Aponyi boy'
referred to was the son of a Hungarian aristocrat.
[112] Alex May, Asquith, Julian Edward George, Second Earl of Oxford
and Asquith http://www.oxforddnb.com/templates/article.
jsp?articleid=103465&back=.

Shrewring, a former pupil of Bristol Grammar School and Scholar of Corpus Christi, Oxford, was an outstanding classical scholar. He won the Craven Scholarship and the Chancellor's Prize for Latin Prose. A Catholic convert, he was persuaded by Fr Paul to leave Oxford to teach at Ampleforth. With someone like Shewring on the staff, it could not be said that Ampleforth lacked teachers of the calibre to be found at Eton, Winchester and the other major public schools. Fr Paul used to tell boys he saw coming from the Classics Room that it was a luxury to be taught by Mr Shewring.[113]

Knox's reaction to Shrewing's appointment is of some interest. He would have preferred Fr Paul to appoint another young Oxford classicist, Lawrence Eyre, who had been offered a post at Stonyhurst. He wrote:

> When I first heard you had taken Shewring on, I felt that it was the wrong way round: that Lawrence was the person you wanted and Shewring the person who ought to go to Stonyhurst, At least I have the impression, I do not know why, that the Stonyhurst boys are much easier to intimidate and that Shewring would have a better chance there. I wish you could trade them.[114]

It is revealing that he did not regard the less disciplined demeanour of Ampleforth boys, the product, presumably, of Fr Paul's more relaxed view of the freedom which might be extended to boys, as making Ampleforth anything less of a school than Stonyhurst; if anything, the reverse. With regard to the teaching careers of Shewring and Eyre, the latter eventually joined the former at Ampleforth, where both enjoyed success. Walter Shewring taught at Ampleforth for nearly sixty years, during which time he became an intimate of Eric

---

113 This comment is included in an obituary of Walter Shewring written by his former pupil and successor as senior Classics master at Ampleforth, Philip Smiley. *Ampleforth Journal*, 95/2 (1990), p. 80.

114 Ampleforth Abbey Archives, DX65, Fr R. A. Knox to Fr Paul Nevill, 25 April 1928. Walter Shewring, notwithstanding his diffident manner, flourished at Ampleforth. He taught there until the 1980s and on retirement lived within the community. He was later joined on the staff by Lawrence Eyre, who became Fr Knox's literary executor.

Gill and his circle, a distinguished Italian scholar (awarded the Italian Republic's Order of Merit in 1978), a musicologist, writer on aesthetics, poet and translator (translating for the Oxford University Press its edition of *The Odyssey*).[115]

Knox gave further assistance to Ampleforth by advising Fr Paul on the placing of his students in the scholarship examinations and in cultivating the school's reputation with the colleges. In a letter of 1928, Fr Paul was advised not to push boys towards Christ Church because Catholics had not distinguished themselves there recently. Two had been sent down for failing examinations and one for vandalism. On the other hand, the prospects at Hertford were improving. Knox told Fr Paul:

> I dined last night next to the Principal of Hertford: he says this week is not too late for applications: the chances of success are about 1 in 2 or 1 in 3. They've already taken one Beaumont and one Douay [*sic*] boy and have another Beaumont application. But the Principal thinks Ampleforth a better school than Downside or Beaumont and I didn't undeceive him.[116]

Later in the year Knox informed Fr Paul of contacts he had made with Maurice Bowra of Wadham and J. J. Urqhart of Balliol about Ampleforth applicants.[117]

The effectiveness with which Fr Paul cultivated connections at Oxford, built up the reputation of his school and carefully prepared his boys for scholarship examinations to both ancient universities was seen in the record of open award success which the HMI Report on Ampleforth cited in 1945. From 1935 to 1945 Ampleforth boys won thirty-six open scholarships at Oxford and Cambridge and seventeen exhibitions. Of these

---

[115] *Ampleforth Journal*, 95/2 (1990), pp. 80–1.
[116] Ampleforth Abbey Archives, DX65, Fr R. A. Knox to Fr Paul Nevill, 2 May 1928.
[117] *Ibid.*, Fr R. A. Knox to Fr Paul Nevill, 19 June 1928. J. J. 'Sligger' Urqhart was a longstanding connection of Fr Paul's and, it would appear, another friend. Urqhart was a Catholic and in 1913 had requested that Fr Paul be spared from Ampleforth to cover the Oxford Chaplaincy before Fr Maturin was free to take up the full-time appointment. Letter from J. J. Urqhart to Fr Paul Nevill, 26 September 1913.

awards, eighteen were in the Classics, thirteen in history, ten in science, eight in mathematics and four in modern languages.[118] Fr Paul had taken the advice offered by Pickard in 1924 and implemented it with no little success.

---

[118]   Ampleforth Abbey Archives, GX 87 31. 7S 57, p. 10.

Conclusion

A MPLEFORTH COLLEGE, having been one of the smaller and less well-known Catholic colleges for much of its history, played an important role in the integration of Catholic schools within the educational world of the English middle and upper classes: a world dominated by the public schools developed in the course of the nineteenth century. Ampleforth was quick to take advantage of the Church's relaxation of the prohibition of Catholics attending the Anglican universities by establishing a house of studies at Oxford. Ampleforth increasingly resembled an Anglican public school in structure and ethos. This culminated in the headmastership of Fr Paul Nevill when Ampleforth became a leading player in the public school world by winning scholarships to the ancient universities, achieving success on the games field and sending its old boys into the professions. The ability of Ampleforth to attract the sons of the Catholic aristocracy and gentry helped put it in the front rank of the public schools.

In large part, Ampleforth's success in becoming part of the established world of the English public school was the result of the willingness of those such as Fr Paul Nevill to jettison much of the Catholic educational tradition within which the school had grown, both in the days of continental exile and on the return to England. It has to be acknowledged, however, that this Catholic educational tradition was a viable alternative to what was on offer in the Anglican public schools of the nineteenth century. There is a case to be made for the Ampleforth of the 1820s as one of the best schools in the country from the perspectives of the breadth of its curricular provision and the quality of staff–pupil relationships.

There was, moreover, some resistance to the transformation of Ampleforth into an English public school from within the Catholic community. There were misgivings about the direction being taken by the school at Ampleforth in the inter-war period and, to an even greater extent, at Downside in the 1930s. Even after the transformation had been made at Ampleforth, and elsewhere, there were still those with doubts and mixed feelings. Mgr Barnes, who was prepared to celebrate the growing fame of the Catholic public schools, was also aware of something being lost, noted by the *Times Literary Supplement* in its review of his 1926 book:

> Mgr Barnes says all that traditionists must regret in one sentence: The old Catholic tradition of education was very thorough and very solid. In those days boys were taught and men studied in order to master a subject, not as now to pass an examination.[1]

Evennett, provides another example of this type of reaction. In his 1944 book, he acknowledged the achievement of those who had turned Catholic schools into English public schools:

> The grafting, in varying degrees of public school organisation, technique and ways of school life on to the stocks of the older Catholic colleges ... has been a remarkable educational achievement which has not only demonstrated the great powers of adaptation possessed by Catholic institutions but has also illustrated the strength of the English Catholic desire to work, wherever, possible, through national forms and traditions.[2]

However, he also stated:

> It may, however, be asked, not impertinently, whether by falling into line with the scholarship and certificate dominated educational programmes of other English schools, the Catholic schools have not to some extent compromised their basic principles of the integration of the whole educational process around the central unifying point of the Catholic religion.

[1] *Times Literary Supplement,* 4 December 1926.
[2] Evennett, *The Catholic Schools,* p. 120.

He was concerned that Catholic schools had run into the danger, 'as is too often apt to be the case', of creating 'a rather poor imitation of the traditional culture of the English Public School'.[3]

The Old Amplefordian Harmon Grisewood, who became a leading figure at the BBC, also had reservations. Writing to Robert Speaight (in reply to a request for material for a projected biography of Fr Paul Nevill) on being asked what had been gained and what lost by Fr Paul's work at Ampleforth, Grisewood responded as follows:

> In retrospect a great deal was lost — Including the chance of making a real development on the basis of the old Ampleforth which would be intended to yield a Catholic public school instead of a public school of the ordinary sort, the inmates of which happen to subscribe to the Catholic faith and are provided with the facilities for practising it and some encouragement to do so.

In his view, Ampleforth had lost the virtues of its small size, its un-worldliness and its simple provincial piety, 'something the Catholic world was used to since the Reformation'. The old Ampleforth 'may not have been a very good school but it was Catholic through and through. I doubt if the school of VPN [Fr Paul Nevill] was Catholic in the same sense.' In return the gains had been 'An improvement in the standard of education judged by the general national examinations standard' and 'A school where Catholic mummies and daddies and the upper class and richer sort are glad to send their boys whereas many of them might have gone to Eton or some other non-Catholic schools'. When considering whether justifiable compromises had been made by Fr Paul to create the modern Ampleforth, Grisewood's opinion was that 'It's a question of how far it was really a compromise at all . . . As you will have gathered, I don't think VPN's work was really a continuation or fulfilment . . . so much as a lunge in the Arnoldian direction'.[4]

---

[3]   *Ibid.*, pp. 101–2.
[4]   Ampleforth Abbey Archives, BX05–03 7M12, Letter from H. Grisewood to R. Speaight, 6 December 1961.

Robert Speaight did not write a full biography of Fr Paul, but he did produce an article in the *Ampleforth Journal*. In this he echoed some of Grisewood's reservations and added his own judgment from the viewpoint of an Ampleforth parent:

> In the context of English Public School education Fr Paul was neither an innovator like Sanderson of Oundle, nor a progressive like Coad of Bryanston. He took the Public Schools as he found them, and was glad to take them so . . . If an outsider may be permitted an opinion, I think that he allowed the senior boys powers which no boy should be given over another, and that he allowed the junior boys to be plagued with too many puerilities of protocol. But these things were rooted, for better or worse, in the tradition he was resolved to imitate.[5]

It is, however, most doubtful that a Catholic public school substantially different from the schools which Ampleforth, Downside and Stonyhurst became would have been viable propositions: schools capable of attracting the children of prosperous Catholic families. Of these schools, the one which changed the least in the matter of giving up traditional Catholic educational structures was Stonyhurst, and, arguably, this was the Catholic school, from the perspectives of numbers and social standing, which did least well in the twentieth century, losing its leading position in the world of Catholic independent schools to its Benedictine rivals.[6] Whatever the

[5] *Ampleforth Journal*, 92 (1987), p. 4.
[6] The schools that most strongly retained the characteristics of the Catholic educational tradition were the urban grammar schools run by orders such as The Christian Brothers and the De La Salle Order (The Brothers of the Christian Schools). Largely catering for the sons of the lower middle class and skilled working class, their adoption of the ethos and structures of the English public schools was the palest of imitations. As late as the 1960s, De La Salle schools still had 'brother directors' rather than headmasters and still employed 'masters in charge of discipline'. Sixth-form prefects had few of the responsibilities or powers of their public-school counterparts. On De La Salle schools, see W. J. Battersby, *The De La Salle Brothers in Great Britain* (London: Burns and Oates, 1954) and, for the author's own school, M. Magan, *Cradled in History, St John's College, Southsea, 1908–1976* (Portsea: St John's College, 1976).

strengths of the Catholic educational tradition (the meticulous scholarship, the curricular breadth, the limited scope for boys to bully their fellows, the concern with learning for its own sake rather than an obsession with passing public examinations, the teaching of lay and secular pupils side-by-side and the locating of the school's life firmly within the sacramental life of the Church), this tradition was not strong enough to be kept alive in isolation from wider national developments. Attempts to keep the Catholic Church, especially in its educational arrangements, wholly separate were doomed to failure. Bishop Baines could not make his scheme for a combined school seminary and university as the apex of a Catholic educational system work; neither could Cardinal Manning's plans for a Catholic university at Kensington be brought to fruition. The ruling elite in nineteenth-century Britain, with the glaring exception of Ireland, was remarkably successful in creating consent to its institutions amongst classes and communities that might be alienated from the established order. For example, political reform, economic success and the creation of an empire all combined to take the sting out of the working-class radicalism of the early nineteenth century and militant Nonconformity. The overwhelming majority in later-nineteenth-century Britain wanted to identify with rather than against most of the institutions of the established order. The Anglican public schools, and the ancient universities, were significant elements of this established order and their notions of what it was to be an English gentleman and a scholar were dominant values.

The Catholic gentry and the growing Catholic middle class, especially the professional middle class, wanted access to the type of education enjoyed by their Anglican equivalents. This was also the case with middle-class Nonconformists and their schools followed a similar path to that taken by Ampleforth. Caterham School, for example, founded in 1811 as a school for the sons of Congregationalist ministers, existed throughout the nineteenth century as a small boarding school separate from the world of the Anglican public schools. Its headmaster from 1910 to 1934, A. P. Mottram, created a sixth form, introduced the house system and brought in rugby. In 1924 he was elected to the HMC.[7] The difference between Ampleforth and Caterham, and the other Nonconformist schools, however, was in the matter of the social standing of their intakes. Ampleforth, with its aristocratic and gentry element, could rank with the leading schools. The Nonconformist schools, whatever their academic and sporting achievements, lacked such social cachet.

The role of the public schools in shaping middle-class attitudes from the late Victorian period has been pointed out by modern social historians. In an analysis of middle-class approaches to marriage in the last quarter of the nineteenth century, Thompson argued that upper middle-class parents saw public school men as ideal matches for their daughters:

> Having been to a public school was the necessary, instantly recognizable, stamp of approval in situations where contacts between young people were becoming less and less confined to the older enclosed and cloistered circles in which parental families were well acquainted with one another through the long familiarity of cousinhood, shared neighbourhood, shared religion, or common profession. It was also evidence that class was replacing sect or locality as the dominant criterion of middle-class marriage; it was, of course, class as moulded by a particular kind of education and the set of family values which could be assumed to lie behind the selection of that kind of schooling, rather than class deriving at all directly from birth, occupation or income.[8]

The point about public schools being agents of the creation of a national middle-class outlook and culture was also made by Harris, when she said that 'the growth of public boarding schools increasingly replaced the old provincial grammar schools and dissenting academies by a new cosmopolitan upper-class culture, largely divorced from local roots'.[9]

---

7 E. de C. Blomfield, *A Century at Caterham 1884–1984* (London: Kiek and Read, 1983), pp. 43–63.
8 F. M. L. Thompson, *The Rise of Respectable Society* (London: Fontana Press, 1988), pp. 105–6.
9 J. Harris, *Private Lives and Public Spirit: Britain 1870–1914* (Oxford: Oxford University Press, 1994), p. 21.

On the eve of the Great War there were approaching two million Catholics in England and Wales.[10] Most Catholics may have been working-class and of Irish descent, but a community of this size, besides having a gentry element of old Catholic families and those brought in by conversions, also contained a middle class. Catholic doctors, lawyers, officers in the services and the rest, whatever their disposition and whatever encouragement offered by their bishops to hold on to their Catholic identity, were unlikely to remain aloof from the rest of their class. What was happening to the middle class nationally would affect them. In these circumstances, those who argued for working within the established order by attending Oxford and Cambridge and turning the Catholic schools into English public schools were taking the most realistic line. To stay aloof and spurn opportunities for greater social integration being offered to Catholics at the start of the twentieth century could well have been to condemn the Catholic colleges to decline. Fr Paul Nevill's Ampleforth may have been open to the criticisms of Harmon Grisewood, but these were substantially unfair. Ampleforth was much more than a poor imitation of an English public school. Alongside the house system, the power of prefects or monitors, the focus on winning awards at Oxford and Cambridge, the concentration on games, the Officer Training Corps and the rest, Ampleforth boys continued to be educated by a monastic community. Ampleforth was still clearly a Catholic school. The school day was built around its prayer life, boys continued to worship with the community and members of the community continued to leave the school to work in the parishes served by Ampleforth since mission times. Making Ampleforth a leading English public school had been more than a 'lunge towards Arnoldism'. As the HMI report of 1945 noted, 'Ampleforth is a school of character and distinction. Entering late into the general current of public school education it has appropriated the best features

---

[10] A. D. Gilbert, *Religion and Society in Industrial England* (London: Longman, 1976), p. 46. Gilbert gives the following estimates of the Catholic population in England: 1840, 700,000; 1851, 900,000; 1891, 1,357,000; 1911, 1,710,000; and 1913, 1,793,038.

of this tradition and retains intact its own special and unique elements.'[11]

A good illustration of the synthesis of Catholic education and the English public school tradition achieved under Fr Paul Nevill is provided by the reminiscences of Fr Adrian Convey.[12] Fr Adrian was educated at Ampleforth, entering the monastery straight from school in 1949. From 1964 until 1981, he was housemaster of St Oswald's, where he had been a boy under Fr Stephen Marwood. Much of what Fr Adrian remembered would be familiar to any public schoolboy of his generation. The focal point of his school experience was the house. Comparing his experience with the Ampleforth of 2001, he recalled that 'Each house was very much more self-contained than is the case today. Until you reached the sixth form, you never set foot in any house but your own.'[13] Monitors were integral to the discipline system. Boys could be beaten by monitors and, if a housemaster were absent, the head monitor of the house took over. At the start of each term the whole school would assemble to be addressed by the head monitor and captain of games, and 'listen in respectful and slightly awed silence' to their plans for the coming term.[14] Academic performance was monitored and form order mattered. The hierarchy of the form order determined where names appeared on the school list, seating arrangements for the refectory, house prayers and in church. Sixth formers were privileged and at the top of the school was the scholarship sixth, the boys trying for Oxford and Cambridge. Fr Adrian recalled that in his last year of school a record was set when seventeen scholarships and exhibitions were achieved and that 'In the late forties and early fifties there were about ninety Amplefordians at Oxford and forty at Cambridge'.

Ampleforth at this time, however, was still very much a Catholic school and in touch with its own traditions. Goremire

---

[11] Ampleforth Abbey Archives, GX 87 32 7S 57, HMI Report on Ampleforth, 1945, p. 22.
[12] Fr Adrian Convery, 'Experiences of a Housemaster in Former Days', *Ampleforth Journal*, 106 (Autumn 2001), pp. 73–9.
[13] *Ibid.*, pp. 73–4
[14] *Ibid.*, p. 76.

Day was still observed in June, as it had been since the 1800s (originally, to allow the premises to be thoroughly cleaned) when the entire school decamped to a small lake below Sutton Bank for a picnic. All housemasters and 70 per cent of the staff were monks. Monks headed every department, ran the Combined Cadet Force and all school games. The school day began with mass at 7.25 AM, followed by the whole school being led in prayers by Fr Paul in Big Passage before House Prayers at 9am. After the day's lessons and games, there were evening House Prayers at 9 PM. On Sundays, there was early mass and communion in the houses at 8.30 AM, followed by High Mass for the school and community in the Abbey Church. Vespers and Benediction took place at 5.15 PM.[15] Twice a year there were silent retreats from Sunday to Tuesday and every day the school stopped to pray the Angelus at the ringing of the bell at midday and at 6 PM.[16]

Over a period of thirty years, Fr Paul Nevill set Ampleforth on the path to becoming the Catholic Eton. To this day, his influence is commemorated in the massive portrait by Derek Clarke at the heart of the school building. Having established the school's structures and ethos, Ampleforth's heyday was secured under the headmasterships of his successors. Fr Paul, who died at his desk, was followed by Fr William Price. Fr William came from a markedly different background to his predecessor. The son of Sir Charles Price, a Conservative MP, Fr William Price was a convert to Catholicism. Educated at Radley and Corpus Christi College, Oxford, he had served as an officer in the First World War. He pursued a career in the law and business, working as a lawyer for British American Tobacco in Shanghai before entering the monastery in 1933. In the reminiscences of Fr Dominic Milroy, an Ampleforth-educated member of the monastic community, housemaster and headmaster, Fr William adopted a more detached approach to school management than Fr Paul. In Fr Dominic's view,

---

15   *Ibid.*, p. 75.
16   *Ibid.*, p. 78.

He was never hands-on, keeping a benevolent eye on the whole operation and showing interest in the bid issues rather than the details of administrative paperwork. He presided over the school in a less personal way, perhaps reflecting something of his shy nature.[17]

Even so, Fr William's ability to build upon the foundations created by his immediate predecessor was impressive. The school he inherited in 1954 had been a member of the HMC for less than ten years. By the time of his retirement a decade later, it had increased its numbers by over one hundred and two new houses had been founded. In 1964, five of its old boys were awarded first class degrees at Oxford and Cambridge.[18] Fr William's successor, Fr Patrick Barry, an old boy of Fr Paul Nevill's Ampleforth, became the first Catholic to chair the HMC and see the school's numbers reach six hundred in ten houses. By the time of his retirement, Old Amplefordians were to be found within the British elite to the extent that Heald's contention that Ampleforth was one of the handful of schools that could claim to be major public schools could be made and ensure that whenever Ampleforth's name appeared in the press, or school guides, the phrase 'Catholic Eton' would usually be included.[19] Ampleforth was perceived as being in the upper echelon of the English public school world. Amongst the Catholic public schools, it held a position comparable to

[17] See Fr Dominic Milroy's account of the headmastership of Fr William Price in Marett-Crosby, *Ampleforth*, pp. 83–4. Fr Dominic was headmaster of Ampleforth from 1980 to 1992 and became the second headmaster of a Roman Catholic school to be elected Chairman of the HMC in 1992.

[18] Obituary of William Price, *English Benedictine History*. Available online at www.plantata.org.uk>price>w71.

[19] Fr Patrick Barry entered Ampleforth as a boy in 1927 and the monastery after the Second World War. Before becoming headmaster himself in 1964, he was largely responsible for the fundraising to complete the abbey church designed by Sir Gilbert Scott. He became the first Catholic Chairman of the HMC in 1973. Retiring as headmaster in 1980, he later became abbot of Ampleforth. His obituary includes the phrase 'Catholic Eton'. *Times* obituary. 1 March 2016. For the reference to Ampleforth as a major public school, see Heald, *Networks*, p. 245.

that of Eton within the wider world. Moreover, it provided the Catholic elite with a means of integration, and promotion, within wider British society, whilst preserving a distinctively Catholic identity.

Bibliography

DOCUMENTS

Ampleforth Abbey Archives.

OFFICIAL PAPERS

Parliamentary Papers. Taunton Commission, 1867–8, XXVIII. Parts vii, xv, xiv, xv.

JOURNALS AND NEWSPAPERS

Ampleforth Journal.
Conference and Common Room.
The Tablet.
The Times.
The Times Literary Supplement.

BOOKS

Allanson, A., *Biography of the English Benedictines.* Totton: Ampleforth Abbey, 1999.
Almond, C., *The History of Ampleforth Abbey.* London: R. and T. Washbourne, 1903.
Archer, R. L., *Secondary Education in the Nineteenth Century.* London: Frank Cass, 1966.
Atha, A., and S. Drummond, *Good Schools Guide.* London: Lucas Books, 1989.
Ball, S. J., *Foucault, Power and Education.* Abingdon: Routledge, 2013.
Bamford, T. W., *The Rise of the Public Schools.* London: Nelson, 1967.
——*Public School Data.* Hull: University of Hull, 1974.
Barnes, A. S., *The Catholic Schools of England.* London: Williams and Norgate, 1926.

Battersby, W. J., *The De La Salle Brothers in Great Britain*. London: Burns and Oates, 1954.

Beck, G. A. (ed.), *English Catholics, 1850–1950*. London: Burns and Oates, 1950.

Bellenger, A., *English and Welsh Priests, 1558–1800*. Downside Abbey, 1984.

—— *The French Exiled Clergy*. Downside Abbey, 1986.

Bence-Jones, M., *The Catholic Families*. London: Constable, 1995.

Berry, A., *Belmont Abbey, Celebrating 150 Years*, Leominster: Gracewing, 2012.

Blomfield, E. de C., *A Century at Caterham 1884–1984*. London: Kiek and Read, 1983.

Buscot, W., *History of Cotton College*. London: Burns and Oates, 1940.

Champ J. (ed.), *Oscott College, 1838–1988, A Volume of Commemorative Essays*. Sutton Coldfield: Oscott College, 1988.

Cramer, A., *Ampleforth, The Story of St Laurence's Abbey and College*. St Laurence Papers V, Ampleforth Abbey, 2001.

—— (ed.), *Lamspringe: An English Monastery in Germany*. St Laurence Papers 7. Ampleforth Abbey, 2003.

Evennett, H. O., *The Catholic Schools of England and Wales*. Cambridge: Cambridge University Press, 1944.

Fitzgerald-Lombard, C., *English and Welsh Priests 1801–1914*. Downside: Downside Abbey, 1993.

Foucault, M., *Discipline and Punish*. Harmondsworth: Penguin, 1979.

Fraught, C. Brad., *The Oxford Movement*. Philadelphia: University of Pennsylvania Press, 2003.

Gardner, B., *The Public Schools*. London: Hamish Hamilton, 1973.

Gathorne Hardy, J., *The Public School Phenomenon*. London: Penguin, 1977.

Gilbert, A. D., *Religion and Society in Industrial England*. Longman, London, 1976.

Gilbert, P. J., *This Restless Prelate: Bishop Peter Baines*. Leominster: Gracewing, 2006.

Harris, J., *Private Lives and Public Spirit: Britain 1870–1914*. Oxford: Oxford University Press, 1994.

Heald, T., *Networks — Who We Know and How We Use Them*. London: Hodder and Stoughton, 1983.

Honey, J. R. deS., *Tom Brown's Universe*. London: Millington, 1977.

Husenbeth, F. C., *The History of Sedgley Park School*. London: Richardson and Son, 1856.

Joyce, P., *The State of Freedom, A Social History of the British State since 1800*. Cambridge: Cambridge University Press, 2013.

Bibliography

Lambert, R., *The Hothouse Society: An Exploration of Boarding School Life through the Boys' and Girls' Own Writing*. London: Littlehampton Book Services, 1968.

Lawson, J., and H. Silver, *A Social History of Education in England*. London: Methuen, 1973.

Levi, P., *Beaumont*. London: Andre Deutsch, 1961.

Mack, E. C., *Public Schools and British Public Opinion*, vol. II. New York: Greenfield Publishing Group, 1941.

Magan, M., *Cradled in History, St John's College, Southsea 1908–1976*. Portsmouth: St John's College, 1976.

Magnus, P., *Gladstone*. London: John Murray, 1970.

Mangan, J. A., *Athleticism and the Victorian and Edwardian Public School*. London: Frank Cass, 1981.

Marett-Crosby, A., *A School of the Lord's Service, A History of Ampleforth College*, London: James and James, 2002.

McCann, J., and C. Cary-Elwes, *Ampleforth and its Origins*. London: Burns and Oates, 1952.

McClelland, V. A., *Cardinal Manning, His Public Life and Influence*. Oxford: Oxford University Press, 1962.

—— *English Roman Catholics and Higher Education*. Oxford: Clarendon Press, 1973.

McDonald, D. L., *Poor Polidori*. Toronto: University of Toronto Press, 1988.

Milburn, D., *A History of Ushaw College*. Durham: Ushaw Bookshop, 1964.

Muir, T. E., *Stonyhurst College. 1593–1993*. London: James and James, 1993.

Norman, E. R., *Anti-Catholicism in Victorian England*. London: Allen and Unwin, 1968.

—— *The English Roman Catholic Church in the Nineteenth Century*. Oxford: Oxford University Press, 1984.

—— *Roman Catholicism in England from the Elizabethan Settlement to the Second Vatican Council*. Oxford: Oxford University Press, 1985.

O'Neill, C., *Catholics of Consequence-Transnational Education, Social Mobility and the Irish Catholic Elite, 1850–1900*. Oxford: Oxford University Press, 2014.

Ogilvie, V., *The English Public School*. London: Batsford, 1957.

Parsons, G., *Religion in Victorian Britain, Vol. I, Traditions*. Manchester: Manchester University Press, 1988.

Pepinster, C., *The Keys of the Kingdom: The British State and the Papacy from John Paul to Francis*. London: Bloomsbury, 2017.

Reynolds, D., and C. Teddlie (eds), *The International Handbook of School Effectiveness*. Brighton: Falmer Press, 2000.

Rich, P. J., *Elixir of Empire*. London: Regency Press, 1989.

Roche, J. S., *A History of Prior Park and its Founder, Bishop Baines*, London: Burns and Oates, 1931.

Rubinstein, W. D., *Capitalism, Culture and Decline in Britain, 1750–1990*. London: Routledge, 1993.

Scott, G., *Douai, Woolhampton, A Centenary History*, Stanbrook Abbey: Stanbrook Abbey Press, 2003.

Sheils, W. J., and D. Wood (eds), *Voluntary Religion*. Oxford: Oxford University Press, 1986.

Shrimpton, P., *A Catholic Eton? Newman's Oratory School*. Leominster: Gracewing, 2002.

Thompson, F. M. L., *The Rise of Respectable Society*. London: Fontana Press, 1988.

Travers, R. W., *An Introduction to Educational Research*. London: Macmillan, 1978.

Turner, D., *The Old Boys, The Decline and Rise of the Public School* (Yale: Yale University Press, 2015).

van Zeller, H., *Downside By and Large*. London: Sheed and Ward, 1954.

Walford, G., *Life in Public Schools*. London: Methuen, 1986.

Weinberg, I., *The English Public Schools*. New York: Atherton Press, 1967.

Wilson, J. A., *Life of Bishop Hedley*. London: Burns and Oates, 1931.

JOURNAL AND NEWSPAPER ARTICLES

Brazier, Sir Julian, letter to *The Sunday Telegraph*, 19 August 2018.

Chamberlain, Fr L. 'Newman the Prophet—Part Two', *Conference and Common Room*, 44(2) (Summer 2007), pp. 10–12.

Hare, E., 'Michael Faraday's Loss of Memory', *Proceedings of the Royal Institution*, 49 (1976), pp. 33–52.

Heaven, W., 'A Tale of Two Abbeys', *The Spectator*, 4 August 2018.

Laver, B., 'Gregor Feinaigle, Mnemonist and Educator', *Journal of the History of Behavioural Sciences*, 15(1) (1979), pp. 20–30.

McClelland, V. A., 'School or Cloister? An English Educational Dilemma, 1794–1889', *Paedagogica Historica*, 20/1 (1980), pp. 108–28.

Pepinster, C., 'A Gross Betrayal of Trust', *The Tablet*, 18 August 2018.

Pyke, N., 'Can Eton Challenge Ampleforth?', *The Tablet*, 8 May 1996.

Bibliography

Quane, M., 'The Feinaiglian Institution, Dublin', *Dublin Historical Record*, 19(2) (1964).

Snow, P., 'Decadent Decade?', *Oxford Today*, 12(1) (1999).

Turner, G., 'Faith in the Future', *Daily Telegraph*, 1 February 2003.

ONLINE

Douai 1903 to Woolhampton 2003, A Centenary History. Available online at: http://www.douaiabbey.org.uk/centenary-history.html

Douai Society: http://douaisociety.org/History.htm.

English Benedictine History: http://www.plantata.org.uk

Letter of His Holiness to the People of God, 20 August 2018, available online at: https://m.vatican.va/content/francescomobile/en/letters/2018/documents/papa-francesco_20180820_lettera-popolo-didio.html

Oxford Dictionary of National Biography. Available online at: https://www.oxforddnb.com

UNPUBLISHED THESIS

Galliver, P. W., 'The Development of Ampleforth College as an English Public School'. Unpublished EdD thesis, University of Leeds, 2000.

INDEX

Please note that all English schools appear in their own right as top-level headings, while those on the continent are grouped under the various monastic orders that founded them and can be found under 'monks'.

Lightning Source UK Ltd.
Milton Keynes UK
UKHW011238091119
353155UK00001B/4/P